mere morality

mere morality

Dan Barker

PITCHSTONE PUBLISHING
Durham, North Carolina

Pitchstone Publishing
Durham, North Carolina
www.pitchstonepublishing.com

Portions of this book originally appeared in *Life Driven Purpose: How an Atheist Finds Meaning* (Durham, NC: Pitchstone Publishing, 2015).

Printed in the USA

10 9 8 7 6 5 4 3 2 1

Library of Congress Cataloging-in-Publication Data

Names: Barker, Dan, author.
Title: Mere morality / Dan Barker.
Description: Durham, North Carolina : Pitchstone Publishing, 2018. | Includes
  bibliographical references.
Identifiers: LCCN 2018040476 (print) | LCCN 2018045325 (ebook) | ISBN
  9781634311793 (ePub) | ISBN 9781634311809 (ePDF) | ISBN 9781634311816 (
  mobi) | ISBN 9781634311786 (pbk. : alk. paper)
Subjects: LCSH: Ethics.
Classification: LCC BJ1031 (ebook) | LCC BJ1031 .B265 2018 (print) | DDC
  170—dc23
LC record available at https://lccn.loc.gov/2018040476

Contents

III. Humanistic Morality

Introduction

We need a simple way to picture morality. The topic can be bewildering. Hundreds of books, articles, sermons, laws, public policy statements, and university courses have wrestled with it for centuries. It's a sprawling landscape, but does morality have to be so complicated? Is it so hard to know how to behave?

I don't think so. I think we can boil it down to a simple guide. *Mere Morality* is how one former preacher who is now an atheist knows how to be good without God.

In his book *Mere Christianity*, C. S. Lewis attempted to strip away the dispensable or discretionary doctrines of his faith by boiling the essential tenets down to the "mere" minimum that would be shared by all Christians regardless of their denominational differences. I am doing the same thing here for morality, reducing essential principles to the "mere" minimum that would be shared by all humans, not just all believers. C. S. Lewis would not have agreed with me that religion is one of the dispensable complications that needs to be stripped away from ethics, but at least he would have understood my approach.

I am not the first to talk about this. The "harm principle" has been articulated by others. But I am saying it in a new way, offering a novel framework for thinking about moral behavior that can clarify our deliberations as we try to negotiate the tortuous hazards of life with a minimum of harm. My "Three Moral Minds" model does not solve any specific problems. Rather, it serves as a tool that can orient our thoughts as we try to unravel ethical dilemmas. Mere Morality is a compass, not a map. A compass doesn't tell you where to *go*, but it does help you determine where you *are* so that you can head in the right direction as you navigate terrain or ocean currents.

This book started out as chapter 2 in my book *Life Driven Purpose*. That chapter is reproduced here, but is now enhanced with material about the biblical meaning of "evil" and "wicked" gleaned in my research for *GOD: The Most Unpleasant Character in All Fiction*, material that did not belong in that book. *Mere Morality* is now a more comprehensive stand-alone book that shows that not only can we be good without God—we can be better.

In a discussion of morality, religion is certainly fair game. But attacking religion is not enough. Just because I am convinced that holy books are inferior moral guides does not mean I automatically have something better. If I claim we can be moral without God, I need to make a positive case for it.

A Note about Usage

Although it is commonly accepted practice to capitalize the word *Bible*, my personal style is to write "bible," unless it is the name of a specific book, such as the *New American Standard Bible*, or appears in a quote. This is not disrespectful. It is un-respectful. We do the same with *dictionary*, which we only capitalize in the names of actual books, such as *The Merriam-Webster Dictionary*. Note that the adjective *biblical* is lowercase, while the adjectives of actual proper names are not: *Victorian, Darwinian, Grecian*. "The Bible" is a concept, not an actual book. It refers to diverse collections of variously assorted writings translated from different "original" documents into multiple languages employing sometimes variable and even contradictory interpretations.

I quote various English translations, including the King James Version, the New Revised Standard Version, the New International Version, and many others. I mention these translations in the beginning of the chapter "The God Book," but after that, I leave them off the reference. Rather than clutter up the text with "KJV" and "NRSV" after each quote, I leave it to readers to look up passages of interest in their own preferred version.

I

Moral Minds

The beginning of wisdom and the greatest good is taking care to avoid undesirable consequences.

—Epicurus

Why Did I Do It?

I was in the Detroit airport when I saw the baby fall. Heading to New York City to be a guest on the *Phil Donahue Show* in 1988, I was standing in line waiting for my connecting flight to board. I was probably thinking about what I wanted to say on the show the next morning—the topic was life after death—and was not paying much attention to my surroundings. Another group was waiting to board at the next gate, and I may have noticed the young couple in that line. They had placed a baby carrier on top of a luggage cart, about three or four feet off the ground, and the father must have stepped away for a moment.

The corner of my eye saw the baby kick, my leg made a quick stride to the left and my finger tips caught the edge of the carrier as it was rolling toward the hard floor. About a second later the mother grabbed the other side. She would have been too late. "That was scary!" I said. Neither of us wanted to let go for a few seconds, but I finally realized I should give the baby back to the mother. She took the child out of the carrier and held it close.

You should have seen the look she gave her husband.

A couple of minutes later their group boarded the plane. As they were disappearing into the jet bridge, the mother with baby in arms turned and briefly glanced at me with no expression, a quick look that I took to mean, "Thank you." I can imagine the story that mother might have later told her child about the angel in the airport. They didn't know the angel was an atheist.

What I did was not special. You would have done the same thing. Who wants to see a baby fall to a hard floor? Few people would be able to resist acting in such a situation. I surprised myself. It was instinctive and automatic, with no conscious deliberation, as if I were watching someone else. It was immediate emotion. As I was holding onto that carrier, I felt a huge relief, as if I had just saved my own child. My body was on full alert; my breathing and heart rate sped up.

Why did I do it? I didn't know those people. We might not have liked each other. Should it matter to me if someone else's child gets hurt? Was it reciprocal altruism? Did I say to the mother, "Okay, lady, I did you a favor, now you owe me one"? Before acting, was I calculating the risk and the payback, the cost and the benefit? Did I analyze the relative merits of the consequences of acting versus not acting, or consider that I might get sued if I erred and contributed to the injury? None of that went through my mind. There was no time for analysis. What happened was an immediate, apparently subconscious impulse to act. If there were any decision to be made, it would have been whether *not* to act. It was truly a split-second reaction.

Before the baby kicked, I had not been standing there contemplating Jesus, Yahweh, Muhammad, or Joseph Smith. I was not thinking, "What can I do today to bring glory to God?" or "How can I be a moral person?" or "How can I show the world that atheists are good people?" The action was beneath the level of rational moral judgment. It was biological.

We are animals, after all. We come prepackaged with an array of instincts inherited from our ancestors who were able to survive long enough to allow their genes—or closely related genes—to be passed to the next generation *because* they had those tendencies. An individual who does not care about falling babies is less likely to have his or her genes copied into the future.

Suppose instead of acting, I had dropped to my knees and prayed with a loud voice: "Dear God, help that baby!" What good would that have done? Faith is irrelevant to morality. Prayer might give believers the illusion they are doing something meaningful, but it is no more effective than random chance. Prayer is inaction. Believing in God is not the way to be good.

Three Moral Minds

How do atheists know how to be good? How does anybody know how to be good? Should you simply "give a little whistle, and always let your conscience be your guide," as Jiminy Cricket counseled Pinocchio?[1] Conscience is defined as a "moral sense," but what is that, exactly? Is it a physical sense? Do we simply perceive the right thing to do? If so, why do so many people do the wrong thing, and why is it often so hard to know what is right? If our "conscience" is so dependable, why do we need laws? Why do we have moral dilemmas? Jiminy Cricket had a sweet idea but it sounds simplistic, like something you would hear in a movie. How exactly does a "conscience" guide us, and why does it not always work very well in reality? Luckily we are not puppets-turned-human or we would all have very long noses.

Should we follow a code instead? Is morality a lookup list of prescribed rules? Can it be reduced to obeying orders? Should you "always let your bible be your guide"? If so, why do believers disagree about moral issues, and why do so many of them act immorally?

16

C. S. Lewis tried to define a "mere Christianity," a core set of beliefs that remain after all the nonessential doctrines are stripped away.[2] In its place, I would like to propose a Mere Morality, a ground-level understanding of what it means to be good. A well-rounded life will involve much more than the moral minimum, of course, and each of us can choose how far to go beyond that, but I would like to suggest Mere Morality as the starting point. It is a C, a passing grade, a driver's permit. Mere Morality is what allows all of us, believers or not, to get out of class and start living a grownup life out in the real world where the hard moral lessons are to be learned. It is a model, a framework that can help us visualize what we are doing when we make moral choices.

Have you ever seen one of those cartoons where the character is trying to make a decision with a devil on one shoulder and an angel on the other? We often find ourselves torn between what we want to do and what we feel we should do. Since there are no devils or angels, I suggest we replace the image of those silly supernatural symbols of "good" and "evil" with something else. Instead of cartoon characters competing for your attention, picture instinct on one shoulder, law on the other, and reason in the middle. These make up your three "moral minds," and none of them, by itself, tells you what to do. None of them is good or bad. *Actions* are what we judge to be good or bad. Your moral minds are guides that help you do the judging.

Of course, you don't really have three separate minds; there are not three little people fighting for attention in your brain. Just like the Feynman diagrams are not intended to

represent what is actually happening in quantum physics—
they are a way to visually "stand for" the effects—the three
minds of Mere Morality are a way to help think through
moral decisions. Philosopher Daniel Dennett might call this an
"intuition pump,"[3] a tool for critical thinking. Your own mind
is certainly multilayered, with levels of perceptual, emotional,
and cognitive activities (as the story of the falling baby shows),
with hundreds of separate simultaneous functions operating as
modules, or "minds" within your brain above and below the
level of consciousness. Emotion, for example, is more primitive
than reason, and much stronger, but taking all of the different
parts as a whole, we can talk about the aggregate as your one
individual mind composed of separate smaller "minds."

Mere Morality considers the mind of reason to be the
head on the shoulders, with instinct on one side and law on
the other. Instinct and law are the results of minds. Instinct is
the biological outcome of decisions made by the minds of your
ancestors, and law is the result of the collective decisions made
by the many minds of the social group in which you live. Law
can also be the result of a single regal mind, or a small group
of minds, and such nondemocratic governments tend to be
tyrannical, but those laws nevertheless originate outside of your
own mind, and the way to determine if they are good guides
is to use reason. Instinct and law (one on each shoulder) are
past judgments while reason (the head in the middle) is present
judgment. When you are making a moral decision, you have
three "minds" at your disposal: instinct, reason, and law. One
mind is real; the others are metaphorical.

Your three moral minds are not mechanical producers of goodness. They are guides. You can't use them to "give a little whistle" and presto, Jiminy Cricket jumps out with a tiny umbrella saying, "Do this!" Any one of those three moral minds—or all three—can be faulty. Many of our biological instincts are nurturing, but some are thoughtlessly violent. Reasoning may be based on untested premises or inadequate information, resulting in bad conclusions. Some laws derive from primitive tribal fears or the privilege of power and may have nothing to do with morality. In order for any instinctive, law-abiding, or rational action to be considered morally good, we have to know what "good" means. I think the simple measure of morality is the harm principle:

The way to be good is to act with the intention of minimizing harm.

What else is meant by morality? Morality is not a huge mystery. Ethics is simply concerned with reducing harm. (There is a difference between ethics and morality—one is theory and the other is practice—but most people informally use the two words as synonyms, so I will too. Some nonbelievers don't even think we need the word "morality," and they have a point, but I am using the word in the informal sense of "how should we act?") Morality is not a code. It is not following rules or orders. It is not belief or dogma. It is not pleasing an authority figure. It is not "bringing glory" to a god, religion, tribe, or nation. It is not passing a test of virtue. It is not hoping to be told someday that "you are my good and faithful servant." Humanistic morality is the attempt to avoid or lessen harm.[4] It is the only real morality because it uses human values in the natural world, not "spirit values" in a supernatural world, as its measure. It is the opposite of religious morality because it is based on real harm, not the imaginary concepts of "sin" and "holiness."

People should be judged by their actions, not their beliefs. Actions speak louder than faith.

I think most believers are good people. Although religious doctrine is generally irrational, divisive, and irrelevant to human values, some religions have good teachings sprinkled in with the dogma, and many well-meaning believers, to their credit, concentrate on those teachings. Surveying the smorgasbord of belief systems, we notice that they occasionally talk about peace and love. Who would argue with that? Sermons and holy books may encourage charity, mercy, and compassion, even sometimes fairness. These are wonderful ideas, but they are not unique to any religion. We might judge one religion to be better than another, but notice what we are doing. When we judge a religion, we are applying a standard outside of the religion. We are assuming a framework against which religious teachings and practices can be measured. That standard is the harm principle. If a teaching leans toward harm, we judge it as bad. If it leans away from harm, it is good, or at least better than the others. If a religious precept happens to be praiseworthy it is not because of the religion but in spite of it. Its moral worth is measured against real consequences, not orthodoxy or righteousness.

The so-called Golden Rule, for example, is not a bad teaching. It shows up in many religions. Confucius had a version of it long before Christianity, and phrased it better:

"Do not impose on others what you do not wish for yourself." The value of this obviously humanistic teaching derives not from being found within a religious tradition, but from its emphasis on actions, not faith or dogma. Confucius's wording is better than the Christian "do unto others" because it stresses the *avoidance* of actions that cause harm, which is what Mere Morality is all about. ("Do unto others" is decidedly *not* a good rule for masochists, psychopaths, or people with kinky sexual preferences, religious obsessions, or simply bad taste.) Religious groups such as Buddhists, Jains, and Quakers that are known for their ideals (if not always practices) of pacifism are more moral than groups such as Christian Crusaders, Muslim suicide bombers, and Kamikaze pilots, whose dogma has led directly to violence. We can make this judgment on the basis of lessening harm, which is a principle available to all of us.

So the good values that a religion might profess are not religious values. They are human values. They transcend religion, not in a supernatural sense, but in the natural sense that they are available to everyone, regardless of one's particular religious heritage or choice. They are shared across humanity, and what makes them good is their humanism, not their theology. This means that the purely religious values—the ones that make a religion unique and supposedly "better" than the others—are not good values, because they are irrelevant to morality. What day of the week you should worship, how many times you should say a certain prayer, what religious texts you should memorize, how you should dress, whether women should wear jewelry or makeup in church (or whether their bodies should be seen at all), what words you can say or pictures you can draw or songs you can sing, what books you should read or music you should listen to or movies you should watch, what foods you should eat, whether you can drink alcohol or caffeine, whether women can take positions of leadership, if and how women should submit to men, how women should control their own reproductive future, who your children are allowed to date or marry, how gays, nonconformists, heretics, or infidels should be dealt with, how a class of privileged leaders (clergy) should be treated or addressed or whether they should be allowed to marry, how much of your money or time is demanded by the religion, how many times a day you should pray, what words should be said or what direction you should face during prayer, what incantations should be performed during certain rites like baptism and death, what side of the bed you should get out of, what specific doctrines you should believe, what "holy books" or scriptures are true, whether a snake actually spoke human language or a man was born of a virgin, how science should be viewed, whether the earth is six thousand or four billion years old, what was the true nature of the founder of your religion, and so on—all of those beliefs that differ among religions are morally irrelevant, or worse.

Purely religious teachings are most often divisive and dangerous. They build walls between people, creating artificial social conflicts, prejudice, and discrimination. They have started wars and fueled persecutions. One bloody example was the violent Thirty Years' War in Europe, which had many causes but primarily began as a conflict between Lutherans and

Catholics over infant baptism, transubstantiation, and whether prayers to the Heavenly Father need an intermediary.

If religious teachings cause unnecessary harm—and they often do—they are immoral and should be denounced. If we play C. S. Lewis's game and separate out common human morality, Mere Morality, from religion, nothing is left in religion worth praising on ethical grounds. (We might appreciate religious art or music, for example, but this is irrelevant to morality.) Turn it around and strip each religion of its weird supernatural and ritualistic uniqueness and what is left, if anything—such as peace, love, joy, charity, and reciprocal altruism—is Mere Morality, or humanistic goodness.

We don't need religion to be good. Religion actually gets in the way. Getting rid of purely religious mandates makes life simpler and safer. Rejecting religion filters out the noise to bring a clarity of judgment, making it easier to be a good atheist than a good Christian.

Since harm is natural, not supernatural, its avoidance is a material exercise. Harm is a threat to survival. It is disease, predators, parasites, toxins, invasion, war, rape, violence, theft, parental neglect, pollution of the environment, excessive heat, cold, lack of food, water, shelter, and adequate clothing, unsafe working conditions, accidents, drowning, natural disasters such as floods, earthquakes, volcanoes, winds, storms, lightning, mudslides, coastal erosion, wildfires . . . you can add to this list, but whatever you add will be natural. If your intention is to end up with less harm—real natural harm, not imaginary "sin," which is supposedly offending the so-called holiness of a fictional father figure—then you are acting morally. And this is true even if you fail; if you truly intend to lessen harm—and the law, for example, considers intention as much as the actual act—then you will learn from your mistakes.

Intention is crucial when determining the legality or morality of an action. If you trespass on my property and trample through my garden while fleeing from an attacker, I will not press charges. If you do it because you hate my family, then I will press charges. In the first case, I can see that my garden is minimal collateral damage in the overall assessment of harm. In the second case, it is maximal harm, in context.

In assessing harm, it is the overall consequences that matter, not just personal desires. People who are selfish, greedy, and egotistical may indeed be trying to minimize the harm to their own personal lives, but if they are ignoring the harm their actions cause to others, they are not acting morally. That is what morality means. That is why we have laws against theft, homicide, battery, abuse, mayhem, and perjury. Mere Morality does not mean we should completely ignore our own interests; it means we should take *all* harm into account. If an action results in a harm that is much greater to yourself than to another person or persons, then it is not immoral for you to protect yourself. That's why we allow for the motive of self-defense in a trial.

On the other hand, although it might be unwise and unhealthy for you to choose to harm *yourself*, the question of whether it is moral only arises if it affects other people. If you burn a $100 bill that you own, that might be stupid, but it is not theft. If you burn *my* $100 bill, it is immoral. Morality is social. (In my book *Free Will Explained,* I show how moral accountability and free will emerge only from a social framework.) Harm is still harm, whether it is social or not, but your body is your body, and if you are mentally healthy, and if your action does not affect others, and if you can cover your own health expenses, then harming yourself is a health issue for you alone, not a moral issue for society. It should be none of my business what you do to yourself. (Although, if you are my friend, I may try to talk you out of it.) If a man cuts off one of his own fingers (or some other body part, as Jesus encouraged in Matthew 19:11–12[5]),that is certainly harmful and destructive, and may be unhealthy, but the act is only *immoral* if it affects other people—and it might indeed, especially if others are dependent on that person. (In my case, as a professional pianist, it would certainly affect others.) If I know in advance that that man is intending to lose a finger, and I suspect there is no good reason for it, then I am the one faced with the moral question of whether I should try to stop him. I certainly want to keep people from harming themselves, and I think most of us feel that way. But if the person is not mentally unhealthy, then what he is doing might actually be a moral act, as in the case of the men who shot off their trigger fingers in order to avoid being drafted to fight in a war not of their choosing, preferring to stay home and raise their families. Similarly, virtually all women who choose to have an abortion are making a mentally healthy and rational choice, a difficult decision for moral and health reasons. I'm not directly comparing a fetus to a finger, although most abortions occur when the fetus is smaller than the tip of your little finger. Contrary to the dogmatic opinions of the misnamed "pro-lifers," abortion is not killing an unborn baby. (See the chapter "Religious Color Blindness" in *Life Driven Purpose* for more on abortion.) The blinkered absolutist doctrine of some religious groups that "life begins at conception" interferes with moral reasoning.

And, by the way, when Jesus announced that we should cut off body parts, he was telling others to harm themselves. There were entire monastic orders that castrated themselves because Jesus said in Matthew 19:12 that "he that is able to receive it, let him receive it." Every year or so in the United States we read about a man who mutilated himself in order to prove his obedience to Christ. In my opinion, Jesus was immoral to encourage such action.

Mental illness or instability are not "evil" or immoral. The consequences of the actions of mentally deficient people may indeed be harmful, but we put such people in the hospital, not in prison. It is a health issue, not a moral issue. (I expand on this in *Free Will Explained*.) For society, however, mental illness is indeed a moral issue because those who are entrusted with the authority to determine the fate of such individuals have to determine the course of action that results in the least amount of overall harm to society as well as to the individual involved.

So it all comes down to harm. Mere Morality uses the three minds of instinct, reason, and law to judge harm. Improving on the New Testament, we might say, "Now abideth instinct, law, and reason, but the greatest of these is reason." For most toddlers, instinct is central; for most believers, law is central; but a mature and free human being knows that if reason is not the final arbiter, instinct and law are useless, even dangerous. The three moral minds have to cooperate. Remember, I'm not suggesting you have three little minds within your own brain, only that instinct and law are the results of minds other than your own. Instinct and law prejudge your actions, but reason, the real-time investigator, can re-judge them, using the harm principle as the measure. All three of these tools, taken together, can make a powerful arsenal for moral decisions. For better or worse, they are all we have.

Instinct

The first moral mind, on the left shoulder, is instinct. When I caught that falling baby it was a physical, biological impulse. There was no time for conscious reasoning, but there must have been some quick subconscious calculation. Obviously, my brain had to grasp the situation, "concluding" that a harm was about to occur, anticipating what would have happened if nobody intervened. I put "concluding" in quotes because it seems weird to think of the subconscious mind deliberating to reach a logical conclusion, though something like that must have happened. I must have instantly surveyed the space around me and known it was clear enough and close enough for me to act. But I don't remember any of that. Everything unfolded before I thought about it, below the level of consciousness. Some might call the subconscious decision to act "premoral" or "prerational," but whatever you call it, it worked. The point is that it had to be quick. "An immediate reflexive action," writes Robert Burton, "has clear evolutionary benefits over more time-consuming conscious perception and deliberation."[6] Speed of action gave an edge to those ancestors of ours who became successful enough to breed and raise successful offspring. It is one of the reasons you are here. It is a direct inheritance from your long-forgotten multi-great-grandparents, and if you have children it is part of what you will bequeath to them. Those instincts increase the odds of survival.

On its face that sounds cold and impersonal, as if evolution were simply a massive calculating machine, but inside my mind, inside my body, it *feels* like caring. I experienced compassion when I grabbed that baby carrier. And the fact that it feels good is part of the mechanism for propagating life. We now know that acts of charity and compassion actually boost pleasure chemicals in the brain, similar to how we feel when eating chocolate, listening to music, making love, or laughing. Why do you hold the door open for the person coming behind you? It's partly learned common courtesy, but it's more than that. You don't know that person, and might not even like that person. It's not just reciprocal altruism—"Listen, buddy, you better hold the door for *me* next time!"—because you would do it anyway. You would feel bad not doing it. Why? Part of it is pure instinct, part of it is chosen social cooperation, and part of it is the little chemical kick in the head when you help others. We crave doing good, most of us. "These good acts give us pleasure," wrote Thomas Jefferson, "but how happens it that they give us pleasure? Because nature hath implanted in our breasts a love of others, a sense of duty to them, a moral instinct, in short, which prompts us irresistibly to feel and to succor their distresses."[7]

Thomas Jefferson was a deist, living just like an atheist with no religious practices, but believing there had to be some kind of starter god, or impersonal force that got everything going. The deists were the pre-Darwinian freethinkers, lacking a model for the origin of life. But Jefferson got it right about instincts, anticipating the theory of evolution by many decades. Charles Darwin famously wrote:

> It has, I think, now been shewn that man and the higher animals, especially the Primates, have some few instincts in common. All have the same senses, intuitions, and sensations,—similar passions, affections, and emotions, even the more complex ones, such as jealousy, suspicion, emulation, gratitude, and magnanimity; they practise deceit and are revengeful; they are sometimes susceptible to ridicule, and even have a sense of humour; they feel wonder and curiosity; they possess the same faculties of imitation, attention, deliberation, choice, memory, imagination, the association of ideas, and reason, though in very different degrees. The individuals of the same species graduate in intellect from absolute imbecility to high excellence. They are also liable to insanity, though far less often than in the case of man.[8]

Scientists today continue to prove that Darwin and Jefferson were right. We are discovering that the same "moral instincts" are found in other animals, though to different degrees, as Darwin noticed. All species have evolved instincts that enhance the survival of their genes—they wouldn't be here otherwise—and this often involves behavior that is cooperative, altruistic, and sacrificial. Frans de Waal, in his book *The Age of*

Empathy: Nature's Lessons for a Kinder Society, gives many examples of nonhuman animals acting compassionately. Altruism is an evolved behavior that does not rely solely on having a "higher" brain that can construct formal moral philosophies. Chimpanzees will sacrifice for each other. They will lag behind to help a wounded companion, licking their wounds, putting their own lives in danger to protect a weaker individual. They work together cooperatively. They hug and express emotions of love, gratitude, sorrow, and empathy. Chimpanzees are primates like us, but altruism also occurs within species less closely related to humans.

De Waal tells a story in which an underwater mine exploded prematurely, temporarily stunning a dolphin, who began sinking to the bottom. Two other dolphins came to its rescue, swimming on each side of their distressed companion, placing their bodies under its fins and lifting it to the surface where it could breathe long enough to recover. Whales and elephants are also highly intelligent and show empathy for each other. When wolves get too rough in their play with each other, they will back off and crouch and "apologize" to the injured party. Such acts even occur across species. A dog was seen swimming out to rescue a drowning seal. Dolphins were observed ushering a drowning dog to safety. A chimpanzee was seen trying to help a bird with a broken wing fly. There are many examples of animals from one species protecting and nurturing the young of other species.

We know that dogs express moral emotions like shame, or an eagerness to help (such as compassion).[9] Many of us consider our pets to be members of the family, sensitive to each other's desires, needs, and moods. If you have an animal in your household, don't you consider it to be more than just a "pet"? (You can read about our amazing pet cockatiel in the last chapter of *Life Driven Purpose*.) We can't pretend that they are exactly like humans, but neither should we conclude they are completely alien or inferior. All species on Earth share common genes, and since those surviving genes are the result of ancestors in similar environments needing to protect themselves from harm, it makes sense that there would be a biological continuum, a family tree with common traits. We humans are part of that tree.

You might object that the appearance of animal morality is just a thoughtless expression of an automatic instinct and that we could also give numerous examples of animals *not* caring about each other. But we could say the same thing about humans. The fact is that some of our moral behavior is rooted in our genes. (Of course, everything is ultimately genetic, but some features are more hard-coded while others are more flexible, open to modification by nurture and the environment.) I think empathy, however it is described and whatever cluster of genes or brain circuits it involves, is one of those characteristics of a species that vary across the population, just like any other trait that shows up in a rough bell curve distribution. We humans also show cross-species compassion, but it varies. Some people break into tears when they see cruelty to animals, and if you are like my sister-in-law Suzan, you will break into a rage. But others, on the other side of the bell curve, are not distressed to see such suffering. There are also a few people at the tail end of the curve who actually enjoy seeing animals suffer.[10] (You know if you are one of them.) Most of us fall somewhere in the middle. This may be true in other species as well, with their curves shifted one way or another relative to other species. So yes, we likely recognize less moral sentiment or moral reasoning among other animals—or at least behavior that appears moral, because we can't use language to ask them if their subjective inner feelings are emotional or cognitive, or a mix like ours— but we do see some. The fact that some human animals are uncaring sociopaths and psychopaths does not make us an amoral species.

Many religious believers are taught that other animals don't have "souls" (whatever that means) so they cannot be considered moral in the same way humans are, but that is proving the point. They are agreeing that other animals sometimes *act* morally. Whatever happens in the brains of other species, moral *behavior* does exist, to some degree, regardless of how conscious the individual might be. Some argue that other animals are indeed conscious, perhaps to a lesser degree, but that is beside the point. Instinct is biological, whether there is a "soul" or not.[11] The evidence of empathy and altruism in other species shows that we are connected to a web of life from which our behavioral instincts arise. Many animals have impulses or desires to lessen harm, and humans are no exception. Most of us will instinctively catch a falling baby and hold the door open for the person behind us without much thought.

This does not mean we are slaves to our instincts. "There is no reason," writes Jerry Coyne, "to see ourselves as marionettes dancing on the strings of evolution. Yes, certain parts of our behavior may be genetically encoded, instilled by natural selection in our savanna-dwelling ancestors. But genes aren't destiny."[12] Most of the time we can check our instincts. (In *Free Will Explained*, I describe how we can claim this liberty even though we live in a completely deterministic universe.)

Treating instinct as a "moral mind," or part of the psyche, looks somewhat like the Id in Sigmund Freud's model. Freud admitted there is no such "thing" as "the Id," as I admit that instinct is not really a "moral mind." The Id and the moral mind are both ways to metaphorically visualize the set of hard-wired and soft-wired biological instincts that we are all born with. We have many instincts—some nurturing, some violent—and they often conflict with each other. But Freud did not think the Id was moral in itself. He thought it was something for the Ego and Superego to control. Freud's view was closer to having a devil on your shoulder, while my view is more like having a well-meaning friend on your shoulder—someone you want to consult but not always agree with. I simply want to emphasize that instincts are more than just disorganized uncontrollable impulses. Since the instincts of our social species evolved for a reason, they can be respected as a part of the moral process.

Daniel Dennett, in *Freedom Evolves*, writes that it makes no difference whether our moral impulses are evolved or learned. "[T]he theory that explains morality . . . should be neutral with regard to whether our moral attitudes, habits, preferences, and proclivities are a product of genes or culture." I think this is true because culture itself is ultimately a product of evolution.

Whether you think "instinct" is purely biological or a learned habit, or a combination of the two, it comes down to the same goal: the minimization of harm to biological organisms.

Reason

The second moral mind, between your shoulders, is reason. It is the mind you care most about—what makes you feel you are a free volitional agent—since reason is a function of your own brain, not the brains of your ancestors or the collective mind of society. It is the part that makes deliberate conscious decisions. Reason is clear thinking and logical judgment. Along with your animal instincts, reason helps determine whether or not your genes will pass on to future descendants, not to mention whether you will have a chance at a good life yourself.

In addition to the "lower" dispositions that we share with other animals—and I put that word in quotes because "lower" does not mean "lesser," but "earlier evolved"—we also possess a large neocortex with a recently developed frontal lobe that give us a much greater ability to deliberate before making decisions. (By the way, I think this is a big part of what is meant by consciousness and "free will": the attempt to anticipate the future.) "Humans usually have considered themselves to be different and apart from the other animals," writes Bernd Heinrich in *The Mind of the Raven*. "Perhaps, as lion researcher

Craig Packer points out in his book *Into Africa*, that is because 'we make it all up as we go along,' whereas an ant has 'every small instruction laid out in advance.'"[13] Since none of the other animals have such a proportionately large and complicated brain, they are, as far as we know, unable to construct a formal moral philosophy, but this does not mean they lack altruism, empathy, or moral sentiments. It means they are less flexible than humans, relying more on instinct than analysis. Other animals generally have access to fewer or simpler tools than we humans use in making moral decisions. Your neocortex ("neo" means "new") is a "higher" brain that gives you the ability to reason. (And "higher," of course, does not mean "better," but "with a more recently evolved layer of complexity.")

A useful if overly simple way to say this is that the lower brain gives you instincts while the higher brain gives you reason. That is simplistic because the levels are certainly not starkly demarcated or isolated. They obviously work as a whole much of the time, but it is clear that there is a difference, if only in the fact that the conscious mind is the only part you are immediately fully aware of. If you have time to deliberate, you can use reason to help judge how to act. In fact, you *must* use reason, otherwise you are not a fully aware moral agent.

Reason is not a thing. It is a function of the brain. Our brains have a hugely complex new layer, or set of layers, that have evolved to the point where we now have the ability to use language and to think more broadly about our behavior. We can think about our thoughts. We can think about thinking about our thoughts. We can think about other people thinking about us thinking about their thoughts. (This is sometimes called Theory of Mind.) As I write in *Free Will Explained*, we can deliberate, compare, anticipate, contrast, imagine, and prioritize. We can run "what if" scenarios. We can refrain from acting and wait for more information. (That is one of the functions of the frontal lobe, which checks our actions in social settings. It is what keeps you from burping loudly at a wedding or funeral.) We can investigate, read, and ask for help. We can search our memories for consequences to similar situations, past lessons, previous mistakes.

But all of this takes time. If we don't have the time, we fall back on instinct, or on law (see below), but if we do have time, we can contemplate. An impulse is not always the best course of action. Malcolm Gladwell, in his book *Blink: The Power of Thinking Without Thinking*, and Gerd Gigerenzer, in *Gut Feelings: The Intelligence of the Unconscious*, show that very often we simply "know" what to do intuitively, without deliberation. A hunch can be a signal from your lower biological brain to your higher consciousness that something is wrong, though you can't put it into words. Your "gut feeling" happens somewhere beneath your conscious awareness, but it is no less important than reason. Instincts are a huge advantage, but Gladwell and Gigerenzer also give examples of gut feelings gone wrong. Animal instincts are valuable not because they are *always* right but because they were advantageous most of the time when they were being naturally selected. "I'm not a textbook player. I'm a gut player," President George W. Bush told Bob Woodward about his disastrous decision to go to war in Iraq. Gut feelings can go horribly wrong sometimes—especially when they are prompted by religion rather than evidence—because they are firing in a different environment from which they originally evolved. But we have those instinctive feelings for a reason. Your gut feelings evolved to point usually in the right direction, away from threats, but evolutionary adaptations only need to be more successful on average, not in every single instance. If you want to improve the odds, and if you have time, then you will naturally want to use the newly evolved tool of reason to evaluate your gut feelings to help pick the most morally justified action. Your reason might conclude that your impulse or the law in any particular case might not be the best governor of your behavior. It might tell you that your previous decisions or habits are inappropriate in a new situation. A heroic instinct might be admirable, but it might also be fatal.

What if the falling baby had just been a doll? What if the floor were wet? What if I had lunged for the baby carrier only to break some of her bones, or mine? Or worse? In those cases, my intention would have been honorable but my action might have been counterproductive. I might have injured a bystander. Our instincts can benefit from a careful appraisal of the situation, if there is time. A lifeguard once told me that unless you are a trained lifesaver, or an excellent swimmer with a lot of experience, you should resist the urge to jump in to save a drowning person in a hazardous situation. (If you are like me, you might have a hard time holding back.) Sometimes such actions result in two tragedies instead of one. Call for help. Don't become a dead hero. Yet the fact that most of us have these automatic impulses to do good tells us something about our human nature.

So assuming you have the time to think things through (and you often do), how does your reason determine what is moral? Mere Morality boils down to a simple process: compare the relative merits of the consequences of your available actions and try to pick the course that results in the least amount of harm. That's all there is to it. Try to lessen harm. Of course, there is more to a full ethical life than that—generosity, charity, increasing beauty and knowledge, enhancing health and lifestyle, improving the environment and living conditions, and so on—but when it comes to basic moral dilemmas, use reason to identify the harm and you will know how to proceed.

Morality is not a code. It is a compass. A compass does not tell you where you are or where to go; it only shows you where north is. Think of north as the direction of less harm and south as more harm. If your actions are heading more to the north, then you are a moral person. Of course, you can't always travel directly north—the terrain is often complicated and actions can conflict with each other, and you might have to detour east, west, or even south for a while—but if you intend your general path to go more northerly than southerly, you are a moral person. (No offense to my friends in Australia, Brazil, and South Africa. If you live below the equator, then head south.)

I said above that morality is a simple process, and that is true. It is easy in principle, but usually not in practice. Life is messy. The compass is simple, but the path can be complicated. You often don't fully know what consequences to realistically expect, or how to weight them for comparison. The lesser of two roughly equal evils or the greater of two roughly equal goods can be hard to judge. As I asked in my children's book *Maybe Right, Maybe Wrong,* should I vote for Stinky or Bully? And it gets tougher when there are more than two variables, or when you don't know all the options or consequences, or when you don't have experience with such a situation, or when you are not as informed as you could be. But if you are truly desiring to minimize overall harm, then you will want to learn, to educate yourself as much as possible about what happens in the real world. Look before you leap.

Mere Morality might look like utilitarianism—"the greatest happiness of the greatest number," as philosopher Jeremy Bentham put it—but it is not, because it is at the level of individual social interaction, not society as a whole, nor is it concerned primarily with happiness. Utilitarianism goes beyond Mere Morality. Of course, happiness is what we all want, but I don't think it is my moral responsibility to make you or anyone else happy. My minimal responsibility (if I want to act morally) is to simply try to remove as many unnecessary obstructions as I can from our freedom to seek happiness. (Maybe the mere freedom to seek happiness is a happiness in itself? The old joke asks: "If the purpose of life is to make others happy, what is *their* purpose in life?") Bentham, by the way, was a firm nonbeliever and a proponent of state-church separation. "No power of government," he wrote, "ought to be employed in the endeavor to establish any system or article of belief on the subject of religion." He further argued, "in no instance has a system in regard to religion been ever established, but for the purpose, as well as with the effect of its being made an instrument of intimidation, corruption, and delusion, for the support of depredation and oppression in the hands of governments."[14]

Neither is Mere Morality a negative utilitarianism: the least harm for the greatest number. I don't know if I am capable or qualified enough to calculate the greatest good, or least harm, for the greatest number. How do we assign weightings in such a grand calculation? That sounds like a job for a government (see below), and even governments, with all their resources, have trouble figuring it out.

Mere Morality is definitely consequentialist, although I think it is not just the ends that justify the means. The means also need to be justified by reason: they must involve the minimal amount of harm necessary for the task. That means that the ends *are* the means: the goal of minimizing harm should be accomplished with minimal harm. You might have to amputate a limb to save a life. You might stick a needle into a screaming baby in order to give it a life-saving injection. You might need to neutralize an attacker with harmful defensive weapons. If you are trying to get the job done with the least amount of damage, you are acting morally. That's what morality means.

In his book *The Moral Landscape*, Sam Harris identifies the "well-being" of conscious creatures as the aim of morality. I think that is right. "Well-being" is perhaps a more positive way to characterize the harm principle, but it boils down to the same thing. All through Sam's thoughtful book, when "well-being" is unpacked with real-life examples, they always involve the avoidance of some kind of harm or limitation. Well, you can't be "well" if you are harmed. (Sam and I would both agree that it is the overall harm or well-being that matters, not particular scars or disabilities. If a disabled person is coping well, she may not consider herself "harmed" at all.)

Mere Morality judges actions by their overall results, so I think we should simply call it the "harm principle," and only call it "utilitarian" when applied at a global level. I do recycle my trash, but my action is so insignificant in the big picture that it only makes sense if huge numbers of people do it. This leads us to the third moral mind.

Law

The third moral mind, on the right shoulder, is not located in dead ancestors or individual consciousness, but in the social agreements formed by the large tribe to which we belong. Remember that I am not suggesting that law is actually one of your own minds: in a democratic society, humanistic law is a result of a collective mind (including yours) that expresses itself as social expectation or obligation. Unless you live alone on one of the moons of Saturn, the laws you encounter come from somewhere other than your own conscious mind.

In the "revealed" religions such as Judaism, Christianity, and Islam, humanity is judged by the law. In a humanistic society, the law is judged by humanity. Many holier-than-thou believers strongly feel they are minimizing harm when they fight things like abortion and gay rights. Their church feeds them the dogma that certain things are abominations, not based on any real harm to humans, but on supposedly divinely revealed commandments that declare them to be offensive to the "holiness" of the creator. Their "morality" is otherworldly. Since their principles are not based on real harm, their actions often cause more damage than good. They replace reason with superstition and fear. Reason shows us, for example, that there is nothing wrong with being gay, and if the bible says homosexuality is wrong, then the bible is wrong, not homosexuality. (See my analysis of biblical homosexuality in the chapter "Homophobic" in *GOD: The Most Unpleasant Character in All Fiction*.) These believers are free to have faith and live by their own rules. They are even welcome to try to persuade the rest of us to think like them, but in a secular society, they are not free to impose their theocratic beliefs on everyone else by law.

The law does not originate outside of humanity. The making of prescriptive laws is a human action and is therefore subject to the same scrutiny as any other action.[15] Mere Morality does not require that we blindly follow or respect the law, only that we acknowledge it. Not all laws in the world are democratically decided, and not all laws are good. Many are completely unnecessary, and others are harmful. Moral decisions require freedom of choice, and authoritarianism is the opposite of such freedom. Not all societies progress. Some laws, even in a democratic society, are the result of special interest groups gaining political power and forcing legislators to protect or promote their own narrow agenda. This is especially true with laws pertaining to religion. Whatever country you live in, any law based on "glory" instead of real harm is dangerous. The glory of the nation, or the glory of the monarchy, or the glory of the superior race, or the glory of the church have been the cause of horrible wars and legally sanctioned discrimination. Any laws based solely on these glories should be morally denounced. They cause unnecessary harm.

Mere Morality simply acknowledges the law as a kind of prejudged head start. After looking at the law, reason can judge whether its prescriptions are good or bad in a particular situation. Moral decisions are sounder when they are better informed, so we need to know what the law says. If you are fortunate enough to live in a secular society, one that is progressing via humanistic principles (not sovereign commandments), then the law can be a useful educational guide. The law ideally represents a group wisdom that has already been thought through in advance, based on experiences and data that you might not possess personally. You don't always have to reinvent the wheel.

Most of us rarely bump into the law. If we are reasonable, fair, and kind, we don't need it. The real value of law is for those people who sometimes do not (or cannot) use reason. Criminal law, for example, is largely concerned with correcting those thoughtless instinctive impulses we inherited from our often violent ancestors. Picture the three moral minds: instinct on one shoulder, law on the other, and reason in the middle. If reason doesn't temper your impulses, then law will hop over and try to do it. In other words, if you can't handle yourself, society (for its own protection) will do it for you. But remember that reason sits in the middle: reason can judge *both* instinct and law.

I think I know how to handle an automobile—don't we all? But when I am on a public road, I watch for the speed limit. I realize that the speed limit is not a hard-and-fast limitation of physics, like the speed of light. In most circumstances, I could usually drive safely much faster than the posted speed. But I also know there are good reasons for the state to impose a law on how fast I drive on a road that is owned and used by all of us. I may not know all those reasons. They probably have to do with efficient traffic flow and public safety. In the absence of a true emergency (such as rushing a heart attack victim to the hospital), I willingly surrender part of my moral decision-making to the collective mind of society.

When we say that "the state" is imposing a law, we are not personifying the state as a single person, at least not in democratic countries. The state is all of us, our collective judgment. A democratic government is not a dictatorship, not a single mind handing down decrees. A "collective mind" is not a single group consciousness: it is the result of the pooling and sifting of the judgment of many minds.

"The state" is an idealized concept. In reality lawmaking is often a sloppy power struggle between special interests resulting in compromises, pork barreling, policies based on ideology rather than human needs, and bad experiments that need fixing. I think for many people "the state" is a "thing," attaining a life of its own, becoming a surrogate for monarchy or religion, not truly representing all of us who have entrusted our leadership with the responsibility to govern wisely. But this valid libertarian critique of government does not undermine Mere Morality; it strengthens it. It gives reason a job to do.

Any law can be changed if enough of us agree. We could make the speed limit 100 miles per hour if we wanted to. However, since minimizing harm is a primary goal of traffic laws, the speed limit ought to be informed by science, which should consider such factors as the physics of surface coefficients, the safety features of vehicles and roadways, and the driving habits of the average person—factors which deal with real harm in the real world.[16] The only laws that can't be changed—or shouldn't be changed—in the United States are those based on liberties or restrictions specifically hardwired into the Constitution, such as the freedom of speech, religion, press, assembly, and petition and the limitations on government to abridge those freedoms. Those values are so basic to our lives that it seems unlikely that a supermajority of us would choose to get rid of them by amending the Constitution.

Our collective moral mind has agreed on laws and principles that are good for most of us most of the time. Obeying those laws more often results in less harm. You might be a very good driver, much better than the average, but you can't deny the fact that if something unexpected happened while you were driving 100 miles per hour on a road shared by all of us—if a deer or child ran out in front of you, or a truck swerved due to a blowout, or you hit a patch of black ice—the resulting accident would likely be more deadly at that speed than at 50 miles per hour. The law usually has a good reason. Your individual freedom has to be tempered for the common good. If you don't like that, stay off the highway.

Of course, democracy is no guarantee of morality. If a majority of people in a state lacking constitutional rights and liberties are theocratic, for example, they could vote to limit freedoms—they could use democracy to destroy democracy—not with the intention of minimizing real harm but to protect themselves from the manufactured harm of having their religious opinions challenged. That is why I think the best hope, the only hope, for a peaceful world is secular government.

Breaking the law is not in itself immoral. Humanistic morality judges actions by harm, not rules. Sometimes, as in the case of rushing a heart attack victim to the hospital, it would be immoral *not* to break the law, as long as you are driving as safely as you can. If you get cited for it, well, pay the ticket; it was worth it. But in general, a secular democratic society—a collective humanistic mind—functions better when the harm principle for a particular action can be applied in advance and announced as an expected behavior that on average will result in less harm for everyone. If everybody else obeys the traffic laws, then *you* are safer. If you don't obey the law, then everybody else is at a higher risk, and "everybody else" (government) is morally justified in trying to modify your behavior through penalties such as a speeding ticket, revoked privileges, or jail time.

It often seems silly, but I almost always wait for the walk sign before crossing the street even when there is no traffic in sight. I am not moralistic about it: if I am with someone else who wants to cross, I will go with them. But I do think obeying the law is moral (assuming it is a good law) in the long run. According to Wisconsin statutes, it is illegal for a pedestrian to go against a "Don't Walk" sign or red light even when there are no vehicles within sight, but it seems most pedestrians and bicyclists where I live feel they are above this law. If someone asks me why I stand there waiting, I reply: "If you were in a car, would you run the red light?" They usually say no, but that is because automobiles are more dangerous, and anyway, nobody enforces jaywalking laws in this town. (Try it in California.[17]) But I have sometimes seen pedestrians seriously misjudge traffic and interfere with automobiles. I estimate that less than one person in twenty stands waiting with me for the light to change, and I suppose the nineteen jaywalkers might have legitimate emergencies—who am I to judge?—but I bet they are not all atheists.

I don't think it is immoral or dangerous to jaywalk in every situation. Society—all of us—has acknowledged the obvious fact that jaywalking increases the risk of harm. There are usually good reasons for our laws—if we don't live in an autocracy or theocracy—and those reasons have something to do with harm. If they don't, they might be bad laws. Or they might be discriminatory laws based on religious dogma rather than civil liberties. What sense does it make, for example, to outlaw same-sex marriage or a woman showing her face in public? Those religious laws are simply an attempt to legitimize primitive homophobia, sexism, and sectarian orthodoxy. A moral law would deal with such discrimination by aiming at the attackers, not the targets.

There are many repressive and harmful laws in the world, especially in countries that do not honor humanistic democracy. How do we judge a law to be good or bad? Blasphemy used to be illegal in many parts of America. So was interracial marriage. What about laws related to homosexuality? Or doctor-assisted suicide? What about stem-cell research, abortion rights, birth control, prostitution, polygamy, military draft, tax laws, nude beaches, animal leash laws, motorcycle helmet laws? What about laws based on religious principles? When considering any law, I think we should simply ask, "What is the harm?" If following a law more often results in less harm, we can say it is a good law.

We might disagree about what constitutes a good law or when it might be morally justifiable to break the law, but unless you are a complete anarchist (and I am not dissing anarchism, which might work in small groups), you know that individuals in a large group can benefit from the expectation that all or most members of the group will agree, through voluntary assent or persuasive measures, to cooperate with each other to lessen the risk of harm to each and all of us. It is out of respect, maybe even love for my species, that I stand there patiently waiting for the light to change. It's for my own safety as well because I sometimes make mistakes of judgment. Of course, I am not an automaton. I would be willing, even happy, to jaywalk. If there is an emergency, I will switch from the collective moral mind to my own rational mind, or even to instinct: a greater immediate danger can override any one of our moral minds.

A few years ago, I drove three hours to a debate on morality. As usual, I planned the trip with plenty of time to drive the speed limit (and if I am not able to drive the speed limit, am I really in control?), as well as to enjoy the drive and scenery without being rushed. I was listening to language tapes, so it was not time wasted. I couldn't help noticing that some of the cars that sped past me in the fast lane sported the Christian fish symbol or "Pro-Life" bumperstickers. Perhaps they all had a legitimate emergency, but whatever their reasons, they all felt justified in taking the law into their own hands. During the debate that night I mentioned those speeding vehicles and complimented Christians for grasping situational ethics. (That prompted some nervous chuckles from believers and outright laughter from freethinkers.) For all their talk about moral absolutes, most believers know that real-life morality is situational, conditional. Or maybe since there is no Mosaic law that commands, "Thou shalt not speed," traffic laws are negotiable? (Tell that to the highway patrol, or the judge.) Perhaps all of those Christians who sped past me are excellent drivers, but whatever their reason for speeding, their action increased the risk of harm. If they are caught, they should be happy to be ticketed, since they proclaim such a high respect for the law.

Instinct, reason, and law—the three moral minds—are our guides for minimizing harm and living a good life, but reason is the final arbiter. It is true that human nature possesses instincts that are dangerous as well as helpful, and law can moderate those impulses, but without reason morality boils down to a robotic function. Without reason we are slaves serving a master, computers executing a program, soldiers following orders, believers obeying commandments. A healthy functioning society, where citizens enjoy the right to the "pursuit of happiness," is one that bases its laws on principles, not authority. It is a society whose motto should be "In Reason We Trust."

Pains and Penalties

Annie Laurie and I were married in 1987 by a judge in a secular wedding at Freethought Hall in Sauk City, Wisconsin. We planned everything to represent our natural freethought views of equality, as well as our love and respect for our families in *this* world, not some imagined supernatural world. My Mom beautifully sang "Embraceable You" in that acoustically pleasing historic building, a song written by the nonbelieving Gershwin brothers. Judge Moria Krueger (who says she owed her judgeship to the fact that Annie Laurie spearheaded the successful grassroots recall of her predecessor, Judge Archie Simonson, because of his sexist "boys will be boys" defense of a group of high-school gang rapists) performed the egalitarian, feminist ceremony. Annie Laurie kept her birth name, as did I.

So it was a shock to be confronted by the government with religion when we went to the Dane County Courthouse to get our marriage license. The county clerk asked us to raise our right hands for the oath: "Do you solemnly swear that the testimony you shall give in this matter shall be the truth, the whole truth and nothing but the truth, so help you God?" We were caught off guard! We told the clerk that we are atheists, and reminded her that the state allows for a secular affirmation in place of a religious oath.

"Oh," she said, fumbling through her notes. "No one has asked that before." After a half-minute, she said, "Well, do you affirm to tell the truth, so help you God?"

We laughed. "We don't believe in God," we repeated slowly, "so we can't say that!"

She took a moment to look through the statutes, and finally found the alternative wording in 906.03(3): "Do you solemnly, sincerely and truly declare and affirm that the testimony you shall give in this matter shall be the truth, the whole truth and nothing but the truth; and this you do under the pains and penalties of perjury?"

Finally, a secular promise! We said, "Yes." (Proving you can have law without religion). But isn't it interesting that if you don't believe in God you have to be reminded of the punishment of the law? If you do believe in God you can simply say, "so help me, God," and that is enough to warrant honesty. If you don't believe in God, it is assumed you have less motive to tell the truth, the "pains and penalties of perjury" replacing the threat of "hell" to force you to be a good person. We think the statute should be reversed. The secular oath should be preferred (as it is for the presidential oath of office in the U.S. Constitution), and a religious alternative can be available for those who request it. Besides, the clerk should have appreciated our honesty. If an atheist were to swear, "so help me, God," that would be an act of perjury.

Rebellion

In April 2010, I debated Mat Staver, dean of Liberty University School of Law in Lynchburg, Virginia, on the topic, "Is American law based on the Ten Commandments?" Staver is now chairman of the Liberty Counsel, a law firm defending evangelical Christian values. He later unsuccessfully represented Kentucky county clerk Kim Davis, who refused to issue marriage licenses to same-sex couples because of her religious views. Staver has intervened for the other side in a couple of lawsuits brought by the Freedom From Religion Foundation, so we are truly adversaries, philosophically and legally. The cordial debate took place in their law school's Supreme Courtroom, designed to be a replica of the United States Supreme Court. During the debate, I joked that I coveted that room, but then realized that would be a crime. Trying to connect the dots between American law and the Ten Commandments, Staver mentioned the theocratic laws of the early colonists, Sunday "blue laws," the importance of the bible in swearing an oath in court (perjury laws coming straight from scripture, he claimed), and so on. Abandoning the stated debate topic, he argued that

American law is merely "influenced by," not based on, the Ten Commandments. (So I won the debate by default.)

I pointed out that only three of the Ten Commandments—killing, perjury, and theft—have any relevance to modern American law. "If you get 30 percent on your final exam," I asked the students, "what kind of a grade is that?" My opening statement included these words:

> I am going to break the law, and I want all of you to witness. The god of the bible, if he exists, is an evil, immoral, selfish, arrogant, jealous, brutal, bloodthirsty bully, and if he created hell, he can go to hell. I am not saying, "God Damn It," I am saying, "Damn God." There. I just broke the Third Commandment. I took the name of the Lord Your God in vain. Are you going to have me arrested for blasphemy?[18]

Mat, after complaining that my statement was insulting and shocking, agreed that I should not be arrested for blasphemy in a country that protects free speech. He admitted that there is no law or maxim that the United States should be based on the Ten Commandments, that he would not favor enacting such laws, and that the United States should not become a theocracy. He was making my case: American law is *not* based on the bible.[19]

Law does not need or have "a basis." It has ancestors. There is no object or document out there upon which the law rests. Law—good law, humanistic law—is continuously evolving from earlier experiments as a society improves. Societies don't always improve, of course, but when they do, the adoption of just and fair laws is one of the ways we know it. There used to be a time in our nation when racism, sexism, and classism were perfectly natural and legal—slavery, denying the vote to women, privileged inequality, for example (which are biblically based)—but through struggle and experiment, we have abandoned those primitive harmful practices. Much of that struggle was against the church. Useful laws are not handed to us from outside the universe, written on divinely inscribed slabs of stone. They are human creations.

Good law stems from rebellion, not revelation. The Roman plebeians revolted against the patricians (in the "Conflict of the Orders"), protesting the abuses of power, and came to a negotiated understanding of equality under the law, due process, innocence until proven guilty, and so on, long before they had contact with Christianity or the Ten Commandments. The laws that arose from the struggle to increase fairness and reduce harm were humanistic, not religious. When they were codified, they were written down not by edict, but with reason.

For some strange reason, twenty-first-century theocrats in the United States are fond of referring to the Magna Carta as a religious basis of our Constitution. It was no such thing. It was an ancestor of modern law, much like the little mammals scurrying for survival during the age of dinosaurs were primitive ancestors of the human race. The Magna Carta was the product of thirteenth-century barons rebelling against the authority and excesses of the king, and although it contained some formalistic introductory religious wording, it made no reference to the Commandments or the bible as its "basis." There is nothing in the bible about habeas corpus or due process, for example. Most of the laws in the Magna Carta are irrelevant to Christianity—such as deciding where bridges should be built, or where you can fish in the Thames, or how much knights should be paid—and although a few sections roughly parallel teachings found in the bible (and it would be surprising if they did not, back in those times), no scripture verse is ever cited as a basis for the law. The Magna Carta does not say anything about rights being granted by a creator. In fact, it is the other way around, actually granting rights to God: "Know that we . . . have granted to God and by this our present Charter have confirmed . . . that the English church shall be free." American law does owe a debt to the Magna Carta, but not for biblical reasons.

Neither did English common law, another ancestor, have reference to the bible or the Ten Commandments. Thomas Jefferson concluded that "Christianity neither is, nor ever was a part of the common law."[20] It was originally a jumble of regional legal decisions based on common sense and precedent that roughly came together after a long evolution of trial and error. It is not based on written statutes but on the "survival of the fittest" ideas that had been naturally selected by experience. The prohibition of murder, for example, is (to this day in England) not based on "Thou shalt not kill" or any other statute, but on the legal decisions of ancestor judges amassed over time into a "common" understanding of how we should best treat each other. That is why it is called "common law."

Many of the original English colonists in America were fleeing government tyranny. Those who were religious called themselves "separatists" and "puritans" because they were rebelling, protesting the abuses of power and the limits to freedom of conscience. They were Protestants, after all, fiercely anti-Catholic enemies of the "whore of Rome," as the pope was routinely labeled. Although the colonies began as mini-theocracies, later generations exercised their own freedom of protest and evolved into a more secular society with broader liberties for all believers and nonbelievers. Look what happened with Harvard, originally a religious school founded by Calvinists to educate preachers ("dreading to leave an illiterate Ministry to the Churches") that grew into a humanistic institution of liberal arts education. The seventeenth-century theocrats, at any rate, did not found the United States of America. It was a century and a half later when our actual founders, not wanting any part of the religious divisiveness of the earlier colonies, continued evolving into a secular democratic republic. The evolution is so advanced today that there is now no longer any question of whether any of those once-despised and disenfranchised Catholics can enjoy full participation in our country, although that was a huge issue when John F. Kennedy, a Catholic, was running for the presidency, prompting him to assure us: "I believe in an America where the separation of church and state is absolute."[21] Today, for better or worse, snubbing the religious laws of the Pilgrims, six of the nine justices on the U.S. Supreme Court today are Roman Catholics.

The United States of America was not birthed in prayer, as

the religious right repeatedly claims. It was birthed in protest. We kicked the king, dictator, master, sovereign, and Lord out of our affairs, turning government upside down, making "We, the people" the supreme authority. Our Declaration of Independence, which does not govern our country but did present the rationale for rebellion, states emphatically and unbiblically that the power of government is not derived from anything other than "the consent of the governed." American law is not based on any scripture. We produced a completely godless constitution, the first in history to separate religion and government. Written under George Washington, approved by the Senate, and signed by John Adams in 1797, the Treaty of Tripoli says quite clearly: "The Government of the United States is not in any sense founded on the Christian religion." (What part of the phrase "in any sense" don't modern Christian theocrats understand?) U.S. laws do not stem from commandments revealed by a cosmic authority or sovereign monarch. The constitution arose naturally from a group of people struggling to be *free* of authority, not to submit to rules. American citizens are not subjects.[22] We are a proudly rebellious people.

Yet there remain free citizens in this country who want us to forsake evolved progressive reforms and drag us back to the tradition of servitude. They think it is dangerous to acquiesce to secular laws forged in rebellion: they want us to return to the primitive days of submission to the commandments of a dictator. Law does not mean the same thing to biblical Christians that it means to the rest of us. Their law is bible-based, conservative, and stagnant, while humanistic law is progressive and free to improve. Theirs is autocratic, based solely on the command of a dictator, while ours is democratic, based on the consent of the governed. Their rules come from otherworldly values, while our principles are based on this world, where morality really matters. Theirs is a put-down of humanity ("original sin"), while ours is a celebration of who we really are ("Bill of Rights"). Their view of human nature is pessimistic, while ours is optimistic and hopeful.

In *Losing Faith in Faith* and *Godless*, I describe some of the shortcomings of theistic morality, which is based primarily on a might-makes-right mentality. With its threat of eternal torture, inept role models, and a cosmic dictator who is praise-hungry, angry, and violent, the bible offers an ethical system that reduces to the morality of a toddler who fears and flatters the father figure. In most religions, behavior is governed by rules, but in real life behavior should be governed by principles.

In real life, behavior should *not* be governed by the bible.

II

Fear Morality

*Mankind is not likely to salvage civilization
unless he can evolve a system of good and evil
which is independent of heaven and hell.*

—George Orwell, "As I Please," 1944

The God Book

The word *morality* does not appear in the bible. Neither does *ethics*. This is because the biblical judgment of human behavior has less to do with how people treat each other than with how people treat God.

One way to try to discern biblical morality is to look at how "bad" actions are described. The words *evil* and *wicked* appear more than a thousand times in English bibles, split roughly equally, depending on which version you read. In *GOD: The Most Unpleasant Character in All Fiction*, I point out that most of the time *evil* and *wicked* appear in Hebrew scripture, they are concerned mainly with idolatry, worshiping other gods, and disobedience. They much less often deal with what you and I would consider moral—how to treat other human beings.

Translators often treat *evil* and *wicked* as synonyms. For the same Hebrew word, some versions have *evil* and others have *wicked* in the same passage. Look at Deuteronomy 13:11: "Then all Israel shall hear and be afraid, and never again do any such wickedness." This is the New Revised Standard Version (NRSV). The King James Version (KJV), English Standard

Version (ESV), and Complete Jewish Bible (CJB) also have "wickedness," but the New International Version (NIV), New Century Version (NCV), and Contemporary English Version (CEV) have "evil" for the same word in that verse.

In the famous 2 Chronicles 7:14—"If my people which are called by my name . . . will turn from their wicked ways"—the KJV, NRSV, New American Standard Bible (NASB), and NIV have "wicked" while the CJB and Holman Standard Christian Bible (HCSB) have "evil."

In Genesis 13:13, the men of Sodom are called "wicked" in some translations (KJV, NRSV, ESV, NIV) and "evil" in others (Christian Standard Bible [CSB], Common English Bible [CEB], CJB, HCSB). Six chapters later, when the men of Sodom were wanting to have sex with the angels, Lot objected (19:7). In the CEB, Lot says, "don't do such an evil thing." The Wycliffe Bible (WB), CSB, and HCSB also use "evil," while the KJV, NIV, and NRSV use "wicked" to describe the inhospitality of the Sodomites. So the words are generally synonymous.

In 2 Samuel 7:10, in the NRSV, God tells the Israelites that "evildoers shall afflict them no more." In place of "evildoers," the KJV has "children of wickedness," the NIV has "wicked people," and the CJB has "the wicked." The CEB has "cruel people," the CEV and NLT have "evil nations," the ESV has "violent men," and the WB has "sons of wickedness." This shows how much flexibility (and sometimes uncertainty) there is with translation.

Even when the two words appear in the same verse, the translations can vary. In Genesis 6:5, just before Noah's flood, the

KJV reports: "And God saw that the **wickedness** of man was great in the earth, and that every imagination of the thoughts of his heart was only **evil** continually." Most translations of that verse use "wicked" and "evil" in that order, though the CEB uses "evil" and "evil," the WB has "malice" and "evil," and the CEV uses "bad" and "evil."

The biblical authors never offer a specific definition of those two words, so the meaning has to be deciphered from usage and context. Outside of referring to idolatry and worshiping other gods, it appears that *evil* is more likely than *wicked* to be used in the general or impersonal sense of "bad," such as calamity or natural disaster. God and his actions are sometimes described as evil, but I can't find any place where the English translators called God wicked. *Evil* (as a noun) seems to be a loftier term that can stand on its own, or be attributed to deity. *Wickedness* is more likely to describe human behavior: "Turn away from the tents of these wicked men" (Numbers 16:26). There are exceptions, but I can't think of any place where the translation says "the wickedness that has befallen you" instead of "the evil that has befallen you."

Biblical scholar Hector Avalos writes (in private correspondence), "The Hebrew word *ra`ah* is notoriously difficult to translate." The word certainly means "bad," but that can be "bad things happening" or "morally bad actions." It depends on context. "The larger context," Avalos continues, "is a social system of master-slave hierarchies, where any act the master dislikes is defined as *ra`ah*, but Yahweh is fully viewed as justified in sending any *ra`ah* against those who violate his rules."

The biblical writers did not seem to treat "Evil" the way we do today, with a capital *E*, as some kind of immoral metaphysical state. It was more like: If you are in trouble with God, God will make trouble for you.

According to some scholars, the Hebrew word *ra`ah* (evil) could be from a biconsonantal root (*r*ʿ) that may mean "bad quality" or "inferior." (To make things more difficult, it can also generate the word associated with "shepherd.") Another Hebrew word, *rasha*ʿ, has a similar meaning, but is derived from a different root. All of these problems render uncertain the "original" meaning for the Hebrew roots that English bibles render as "evil" or "wicked." The English word *wicked* comes from "wick," which is a twisted string. *Evil* and *wicked*, in the bible, have more to do with being corrupted or perverted from a perfect state than with treating human beings harmfully. They are not words of morality; they are words of uncleanliness and imperfection.

That explains the pre-enlightened biblical prohibition against the handicapped, injured, and dwarfs approaching the altar:

> "For the generations to come none of your descendants who has a **defect** may come near to offer the food of his God. No man who has any **defect** may come near: no man who is **blind** or **lame**, **disfigured** or **deformed**; no man with a **crippled** foot or hand, or who is a **hunchback** or a **dwarf**, or who has any **eye defect**, or who has **festering** or running **sores** or **damaged testicles**. No descendant of Aaron the priest who has any **defect** is to come near to

present the food offerings to the Lord. He has a **defect**; he must not come near to offer the food of his God. He may eat the most holy food of his God, as well as the holy food; yet because of his **defect**, he must not go near the curtain or approach the altar, and so **desecrate** my sanctuary. I am the Lord, who makes them holy." (Leviticus 21:16–23)

"No one whose testicles are crushed or whose penis is cut off shall be admitted to the assembly of the Lord." (Deuteronomy 23:1)

This is not morality. It is righteous discrimination. A person with a defect is insulted as a "desecration" to God's perfection not because of any bad behavior but simply for being physically imperfect. Whose fault is it if you were born a dwarf? The animals that God demanded to be sacrificed to him had to be the most perfect, clean, and unblemished individuals.

You shall not sacrifice to the Lord your God an ox or a sheep which has a **blemish** or any **defect**, for that is a **detestable** thing to the Lord your God. (Deuteronomy 17:1)

When you offer **blind** animals for sacrifice, is that not wrong? When you sacrifice **lame** or **diseased** animals, is that not wrong? (Malachi 1:8)

"When you bring **injured**, **lame** or **diseased** animals and offer them as sacrifices, should I accept them from your hands?" says the Lord. "Cursed is the cheat who has an acceptable male in his flock and vows to give it, but then sacrifices a **blemished** animal to the Lord. For I am a great king," says the Lord Almighty, "and my name is to be feared among the nations." (Malachi 1:13–14)

So holiness has to do with "detestable" and "wrong" imperfection, not with moral character or ethical principles. In today's society, we would consider that "great king" himself to be intolerant and detestable.

Biblical authors are not uniform in their usage of words, but this is understandable. Dozens of writers over many centuries would naturally have different styles and understandings. There are indeed a few passages that link evil and wickedness with human-to-human behavior. The 10th Psalm says that the wicked "persecute the poor" and "murder the innocent" while the righteous "do justice for the orphan and the oppressed." Other examples include Exodus 23:1 ("You shall not join hands with the wicked to act as a malicious witness"), Isaiah 1:16–17 ("Cease to do evil, learn to do good . . . seek justice, rescue the oppressed, defend the orphan, plead for the widow"), and Proverbs 3 ("Do not withhold good from those to whom it is due . . . Do not plan harm against your neighbor . . . Do not quarrel with anyone without cause . . . Do not envy the violent . . . The Lord's curse is on the house of the wicked."). In Deuteronomy 21, a stubborn and rebellious son who is a glutton and a drunkard should be stoned to death in order to "put evil away from you." (Even if gluttony did qualify as evil, capital punishment seems excessive.) Although all of these passages are intended to avoid offending God's holiness (not human values), they do sometimes coincide with modern concepts of human morality. This is no surprise, since the authors of the bible were indeed human beings with needs and fears just like ours. But those verses are a tiny minority in scripture.

Much more often, *evil* and *wicked* describe idolatry and disobedience, which are direct offenses to God, not humanity.

Idolatry

A verse in 1 Kings offers what might be taken as a definition of the word *evil*:

> But you have done **evil** above all those who were before you and have gone and made for yourself other gods, and cast images, provoking me to anger. (1 Kings 14:9)

The biggest sin in the bible is idolatry. This is because the worship of other gods draws attention away from Yahweh, who, like a possessive husband, becomes murderously jealous when his lover looks at a rival. Idolatry is called "wicked" and "evil."

> Then the Lord said to me: Out of the north disaster shall break out on all the inhabitants of the land . . . And I will utter my judgments against them, for all their **wickedness** in forsaking me; they have made offerings to other gods, and worshiped the works of their own hands. (Jeremiah 1:14–16)

> When you have had children and children's children, and become complacent in the land, if you act corruptly by

making an idol in the form of anything, thus doing what is **evil** in the sight of the Lord your God, and provoking him to anger. (Deuteronomy 4:25)

Those of you who escape shall remember me among the nations where they are carried captive, how I was crushed by their wanton heart that turned away from me, and their wanton eyes that turned after their idols. Then they will be loathsome in their own sight for the **evils** that they have committed, for all their abominations. (Ezekiel 6:9)

Has a nation changed its gods, even though they are no gods? . . . For my people have committed two **evils**: they have forsaken me . . . Have you not brought this upon yourself by forsaking the Lord your God, while he led you in the way? . . . Your **wickedness** will punish you, and your apostasies will convict you. Know and see that it is **evil** and bitter for you to forsake the Lord your God; the fear of me is not in you, says the Lord God of hosts. (Jeremiah 2:11–19)

Turn now every one of you from your **evil** way, and amend your doings, and do not go after other gods to serve them, and then you shall live in the land that I gave to you and your ancestors. (Jeremiah 35:15)

The Ten Commandments—which are supposedly God's ultimate rules for living—begin with "I am the Lord thy God. You shall have no other gods before me." Before giving any moral advice about how to treat other human beings, the first four of the Ten Commandments directed the Israelites to remain faithful to their own god. Worship of other gods was strictly forbidden:

> You shall not make for yourself an idol, whether in the form of anything that is in heaven above, or that is on the earth beneath, or that is in the water under the earth. You shall not bow down to them or worship them; for I the Lord your God am a jealous God, punishing children for the **iniquity** of parents, to the third and the fourth generation of those who reject me, but showing steadfast love to the thousandth generation of those who love me and keep my commandments. (Exodus 20:4–6)

The writer of Exodus uses *iniquity* instead of *evil* here in the Second Commandment, but it's the same idea: not worshiping the jealous God alone is bad. (Not to mention that punishing children and grandchildren for the idolatry of the parents is considered perfectly normal justice.) God even announces that his very name is "Jealous":

> For you shall worship no other god, because the Lord, whose name is Jealous, is a jealous God. (Exodus 34:14)

Jealousy seems like a strange characteristic of an all-wise and all-powerful deity. But that's what he calls himself. In a passage about wickedness in Deuteronomy, God strengthens the commandment with the threat that worshiping other gods will get you killed.

If thy brother, the son of thy mother, or thy son, or thy daughter, or the wife of thy bosom, or thy friend, which is as thine own soul, entice thee secretly, saying, Let us go and serve other gods . . . thou shalt surely kill him . . . And thou shalt stone him with stones, that he die; because he hath sought to thrust thee away from the Lord thy God, which brought thee out of the land of Egypt, from the house of bondage. And all Israel shall hear, and fear, and shall do no more any such **wickedness** as this is among you. (Deuteronomy 13:6–11)

This certainly seems to contradict the First Amendment right to worship freely. It has nothing to do with morality. To me, *this* is immoral.

In any religion, it is the spiritual leaders, of course, who denounce their competition. Here is what the high priest said:

And Aaron said, "Do not let the anger of my lord burn hot; you know the people, that they are bent on **evil**. They said to me, 'Make us gods, who shall go before us.'" (Exodus 32:22)

The 44th chapter of Jeremiah makes an explicit connection between wickedness, idolatry, evil, and the wrath of God:

Because of their **wickedness** which they have committed to provoke me to **anger**, in that they went to burn incense, and to serve other gods, whom they knew not . . . Wherefore commit ye this **great evil** against your souls, to cut off from you man and woman, child and suckling, out of Judah, to leave you none to remain; In that ye provoke me unto **wrath** with the works of your hands, burning incense unto other gods in the land of Egypt, whither ye be gone to dwell? (Jeremiah 44:3,7–8)

In 2 Kings, the biblical deity informs us that idolatry and worshiping other gods is "not right." It is "wicked." The "evil ways" of the Israelites were a direct violation of the commandments:

> And the people of Israel did secretly against the Lord their God things that were **not right**. They built for themselves high places in all their towns, from watchtower to fortified city. They set up for themselves pillars and Asherim on every high hill and under every green tree, and there they made offerings on all the high places, as the nations did whom the Lord carried away before them. And they did **wicked** things, provoking the Lord to anger, and they served idols, of which the Lord had said to them, "You shall not do this." Yet the Lord warned Israel and Judah by every prophet and every seer, saying, "Turn from your **evil** ways and keep my commandments and my statutes, in accordance with all the Law that I commanded your fathers, and that I sent to you by my servants the prophets." (2 Kings 17:9–13)

The Asherim were wooden statues of the goddess Asherah who was worshiped by the Canaanites and Phoenicians. According to the bible, the Canaanites were the original inhabitants of the land who needed to be cleared out. The Israelites were the invaders, supposedly called by God to steal the territory as a love nest for his bride. God's chosen people were the outsiders who were mercilessly conquering the indigenous people.

The conquest of the so-called "holy land" was nothing more than expansionist imperialistic genocide. To make the annihilation complete, all images of the indigenous gods had to be destroyed.

When you cross over the Jordan into the land of Canaan, you shall drive out all the inhabitants of the land from before you, destroy all their figured stones, destroy all their cast images, and demolish all their high places. You shall take possession of the land and settle in it, for I have given you the land to possess. (Numbers 33:50–53)

When the Lord your God brings you into the land that you are about to enter and occupy, and he clears away many nations before you—the Hittites, the Girgashites, the Amorites, the Canaanites, the Perizzites, the Hivites, and the Jebusites . . . you must utterly destroy them. Make no covenant with them and show them no mercy. Do not intermarry with them, giving your daughters to their sons or taking their daughters for your sons, for that would turn away your children from following me, to serve other gods. Then the anger of the Lord would be kindled against you, and he would destroy you quickly. But this is how you must deal with them: break down their altars, smash their pillars, hew down their sacred poles, and burn their idols with fire. For you are a people holy to the Lord your God; the Lord your God has chosen you out of all the peoples on earth to be his people, his treasured possession. (Deuteronomy 7:1–6)

The last verse in that passage is clearly racist. Can anyone find anything *moral* in these words of ethnic cleansing?

Some commentators and apologists claim that the Canaanites deserved their punishment because they engaged in horribly depraved practices like child sacrifice. They offer these verses as proof:

And they caused their sons and their daughters to pass through the fire, and used divination and enchantments, and sold themselves to do **evil** in the sight of the Lord, to provoke him to anger. (2 Kings 17:17)

And he made his son pass through the fire, and observed times, and used enchantments, and dealt with familiar spirits and wizards: he wrought much **wickedness** in the sight of the Lord, to provoke him to anger. (2 Kings 21:6)

We don't really know what "pass through the fire" means. It might mean that they burned their children as a sacrifice. But since it says "pass *through*," it could also refer to a ritual where they had to jump through flames, or walk on coals, or run a gauntlet of torches. In context, we see that the verses also mention divination, enchantments, spirits and wizards, which are also called "evil" and "wicked." God was condemning the actions the Israelites were doing in imitation of the Canaanites, who worshiped the god Baal, as the writer tells us two verses earlier: "They went after false idols and became false; they followed the nations that were around them, concerning whom the Lord had commanded them that they should not do as they did." (2 Kings 17:15) The "pass through fire" denunciation had more to do with engaging in ritual worship of other gods than with burning sons and daughters. The real "crime" here, the main "evil," is worshiping someone other than the Lord Jealous, not harming children.

Hector Avalos writes (in another private correspondence, where he references his book *The Bad Jesus*): "It is difficult to argue definitively that 'pass through fire' refers to killing or destroying by burning in 2 Kings 17:17 or 21:6. One reason is that the same *hiphil* stem of the verb is used in Numbers 31:23, where it is explicitly said that one should pass through fire what will not burn or be destroyed by fire."

> And anything else that can withstand fire must be put through the fire, and then it will be clean. But it must also be purified with the water of cleansing. And whatever cannot withstand fire must be put through that water. (Numbers 31:23)

Even if "pass through the fire" does refer to the "evil" of child sacrifice, the Israelites did the same thing. Read the story of General Jephthah burning his daughter as a sacrifice to fulfill a vow to God in the 11th chapter of Judges. Instead of being convicted of murder, Jephthah was aided by God and heralded by the Israelites. After killing his daughter, he became a judge, led a triumphant life, and was buried with honor. Child sacrifice was not an uncommon event in *any* part of the ancient world. God himself commanded it:

> Moreover I gave them statutes that were not good and ordinances by which they could not live. I defiled them through their very gifts, in their offering up all their firstborn, in order that I might horrify them, so that they might know that I am the Lord. (Ezekiel 20:25–26)

But whatever the reason, the Canaanites were in the way of the conquering Israelites, so they had to be eliminated in a genocidal ethnic cleansing.

> Then Israel made a vow to the Lord and said, "If you will indeed give this people into our hands, then we will utterly destroy their towns." The Lord listened to the voice of Israel, and handed over the Canaanites; and they utterly destroyed them and their towns. (Numbers 21:2–3)

> But as for the towns of these peoples that the Lord your God is giving you as an inheritance, you must not let anything that breathes remain alive. You shall annihilate them. (Deuteronomy 20:16–17)

> The Lord your God will clear away these nations before you little by little . . . until they are destroyed. He will hand their kings over to you and you shall blot out their name from under heaven; no one will be able to stand against you, until you have destroyed them. The images of their gods you shall burn with fire. (Deuteronomy 7:21–25)

You must demolish completely all the places where the nations whom you are about to dispossess served their gods, on the mountain heights, on the hills, and under every leafy tree. Break down their altars, smash their pillars, burn their sacred poles with fire, and hew down the idols of their gods, and thus blot out their name from their places. (Deuteronomy 12:2–3)

When my angel goes in front of you, and brings you to the Amorites, the Hittites, the Perizzites, the Canaanites, the Hivites, and the Jebusites, and I blot them out, you shall not bow down to their gods, or worship them, or follow their practices, but you shall utterly demolish them and break their pillars in pieces . . . They shall not live in your land, or they will make you sin against me; for if you worship their gods, it will surely be a snare to you. (Exodus 23:23–24,33)

In *GOD: The Most Unpleasant Character in All Fiction,* I give dozens more passages of genocide and ethnic cleansing that was commanded, condoned, and/or committed by God. The justification for the slaughter of entire peoples is not that they were immoral, but that they worshiped the wrong god. If the bible were truly a "good book," then *these* passages would be denounced as evil. Instead, *evil* is reserved for those people who choose to think for themselves, to allow religious diversity, and to refuse to endorse violence in defense of the fragile and jealous ego of a racist dictator who demands to be loved at all costs.

This is one of the reasons my mother stopped teaching Sunday School. When she realized what kind of moral example she was presenting to children, she was horrified. "I'm nicer than God," she said when she rejected the immorality of faith and became an atheist.

The Sabbath

Another huge "evil" in the bible is failure to keep the sabbath. Honoring the sabbath is the fourth of the Ten Commandments (depending which version you use). It is the final non-moral ritual commandment before the six that deal with human-to-human behavior. It must be extremely important to God to be included in the list that was supposedly inscribed by his own finger on stone tablets (Exodus 31:18). In addition to the prohibition against idolatry and worshiping other gods, not setting aside one day a week to worship God is very, very bad.

Remember the sabbath day, and keep it holy. (Exodus 20:8)

This might look like a harmless ritual, a way to honor the holiness of God (if you believe in such a thing) by setting aside time to praise him and ponder his commandments. But it is worse than that. Failure to observe the sabbath earns the death penalty.

> You shall keep the sabbath, because it is holy for you; everyone who profanes it shall be put to death; whoever does any work on it shall be cut off from among the people. (Exodus 31:14)

> Six days shall work be done, but on the seventh day you shall have a holy sabbath of solemn rest to the Lord; whoever does any work on it shall be put to death. (Exodus 35:2)

"Put to *death*"? Why in the world would something like this be so essential? What does the sabbath have to do with moral living? Why is it a capital crime? This commandment is *so* important to God—one of the grand rules of life—that if you disobey it, you are called "evil."

> Then I contended with the nobles of Judah, and said unto them, What **evil** thing is this that ye do, and profane the sabbath day? (Nehemiah 13:17)

> Happy is the mortal who does this, the one who holds it fast, who keeps the sabbath, not profaning it, and refrains from doing any **evil**. (Isaiah 56:2)

If you fail to go to church or synagogue on the weekend—especially if you do any work on the "day of rest"—you are a profane and evil person who should be executed. How many believers take this seriously? Well, they should, if they believe the bible is true. Look what happened when someone broke the rule:

When the Israelites were in the wilderness, they found a man gathering sticks on the sabbath day. Those who found him gathering sticks brought him to Moses, Aaron, and to the whole congregation. They put him in custody, because it was not clear what should be done to him. Then the Lord said to Moses, "The man shall be put to death; all the congregation shall stone him outside the camp." The whole congregation brought him outside the camp and stoned him to death, just as the Lord had commanded Moses. (Numbers 15:32–36)

A man was brutally executed for picking up sticks, perhaps to make a fire to feed his family. Is that good? Moses thought it was good. "Of course it is good," some believers will say. "God can do what he wants." The verses that immediately follow this bloody violence tell the people to add fringes to their garments. We just observed a public execution, and now we need to talk about the dress code? Biblical morality is truly senseless.

Interracial Marriage

One way for God to protect the purity of his people's devotion to him was to forbid marriage with outsiders. "Do not intermarry with them," God tells his people in Deuteronomy 7:3. If you do, you are evil, says the prophet Nehemiah.

> In those days also I saw Jews who had married women of Ashdod, Ammon, and Moab; and half of their children spoke the language of Ashdod, and they could not speak the language of Judah, but spoke the language of various peoples. And I contended with them and cursed them and beat some of them and pulled out their hair; and I made them take an oath in the name of God, saying, "You shall not give your daughters to their sons, or take their daughters for your sons or for yourselves. Did not King Solomon of Israel sin on account of such women? Among the many nations there was no king like him, and he was beloved by his God, and God made him king over all Israel; nevertheless, foreign women made even him to sin. Shall we then listen to you and do all this great **evil** and act treacherously against our God by marrying foreign women?" . . . Thus I cleansed them from everything foreign. (Nehemiah 13:23–30)

Notice that Nehemiah used the word "cleanse." Interracial or interreligious marriage is polluted, dirty, and evil, according to the bible. The self-righteous Nehemiah got so angry with this abominable miscegenation, that he beat people and pulled out their hair! Is that sane? Would a truly moral society tolerate such nuttiness and meanness?

Malachi calls interracial (or interreligious) marriage detestable:

> A detestable thing has been committed in Israel and in Jerusalem: Judah has desecrated the sanctuary the Lord loves by marrying women who worship a foreign god. (Malachi 2:11)

The prophet Ezra agreed that those who mix with foreigners are evil and guilty of abomination:

> After all that has come upon us for our **evil** deeds and for our great guilt, seeing that you, our God, have punished us less than our iniquities deserved and have given us such a remnant as this, shall we break your commandments again and intermarry with the peoples who practice these abominations? Would you not be angry with us until you destroy us without remnant or survivor? (Ezra 9:13–14)

> Then Ezra the priest stood up and said to them, "You have trespassed and married foreign women, and so increased the guilt of Israel. Now make confession to the Lord the God of your ancestors, and do his will; separate yourselves from

the peoples of the land and from the foreign wives." . . . Let our officials represent the whole assembly, and let all in our towns who have taken foreign wives come at appointed times, and with them the elders and judges of every town, until the fierce wrath of our God on this account is averted from us. (Ezra 10:10–14)

Intermarriage causes a "fierce wrath" of God. Ezra complained about the "faithless" pollution that comes from "mixing seed" with impure people:

For they have taken some of their daughters as wives for themselves and for their sons. Thus the holy seed has mixed itself with the peoples of the lands, and in this faithlessness the officials and leaders have led the way. (Ezra 9:2)

The entire 25th chapter of Numbers is about how God praised the righteous priest Phinehas for killing an interracial couple:

Taking a spear in his hand, he went after the Israelite man into the tent, and pierced the two of them, the Israelite and the woman, through the belly. (Numbers 25:8)

Today we would call this act of violent homicide a hate crime—some might even use the word *evil*—but in the bible it was considered praiseworthy. Phinehas was rewarded with a perpetual priesthood "because he was zealous for his God, and made atonement for the Israelites." (Numbers 25:13)

History is filled with examples of ethnic purges to protect the "purity" of the "master race," even in the twenty-first century. Many countries are still struggling with how to treat aliens, outsiders, immigrants, and foreigners. Xenophobia is an unfortunate inheritance of our tribal ancestry and our "sacred texts," but that doesn't make it right. The human race is a single species on a single globe. Why should there be any "outsiders"? I hope you agree with me that *fighting* these intolerant notions, not embracing them, is part of what it means to be moral. Denouncing the evil of the "Good Book" is a good thing to do.

Disobedience

Of course, it is all about submission. In addition to impurity and idolatry, *evil* and *wicked* also describe disobedience in the bible.

> And you will again see the distinction between the righteous and the **wicked**, between those who serve God and those who do not. (Malachi 3:18)

Here it is clear that wickedness is not associated with morality at all. Those who serve god are "righteous." Those who do not (like me) are "wicked." From the verses preceding Malachi 3:18, we see that "serving God" is about making proper offerings, which were commanded by God. Malachi goes on to clarify what God wants:

> Remember the law of my servant Moses, the decrees and laws I gave him at Horeb for all Israel. (Malachi 4:4)

Biblical morality is about obedience, not harm. Humbly do what the law says and keep your mouth shut. Otherwise, you are evil.

As for anyone who presumes to disobey the priest appointed to minister there to the Lord your God, or the judge, that person shall die. So you shall purge the **evil** from Israel. (Deuteronomy 17:12)

Yet they did not obey or incline their ear, but, in the stubbornness of their **evil** will, they walked in their own counsels, and looked backward rather than forward. (Jeremiah 7:24)

Yet they did not obey or incline their ear, but everyone walked in the stubbornness of an **evil** will. So I brought upon them all the words of this covenant, which I commanded them to do, but they did not. (Jeremiah 11:8)

Mere morality, modern morality, allows for disobedience. Following orders might often be prudent, but it is not necessarily always right. Even in the military, there are times when disobeying a superior officer is allowed, even required. If your commanding officer tells you to shoot an enemy prisoner in the head, and you refuse, that might be a very brave and moral action. An act of civil disobedience for a just cause is often morally praiseworthy. But it is always for a good reason, to protest a greater harm.

However, in the bible there is no room for disobedience of the Supreme Leader. Such insubordination is "evil."

Thus saith the Lord of hosts; Behold, I will send upon them the sword, the famine, and the pestilence, and will make them like vile figs, that cannot be eaten, they are so **evil**. And I will persecute them . . . Because they have not hearkened to my words, saith the Lord. (Jeremiah 29:17–19)

The reason the "evil" Israelites had to wander in the wilderness for forty years was not because they were harming each other, but simply because they did not "unreservedly" obey God:

Surely none of the people who came up out of Egypt, from twenty years old and upward, shall see the land that I swore to give to Abraham, to Isaac, and to Jacob, because they have not unreservedly followed me . . . And the Lord's anger was kindled against Israel, and he made them wander in the wilderness for forty years, until all the generation that had done **evil** in the sight of the Lord had disappeared." (Numbers 32:11–13)

This punishment had nothing to do with morality. It had to do with disrespect for authority.

Even *questioning* authority is considered "wicked" in the bible. In the 16th chapter of Numbers, a man named Korah and some of his followers confronted Moses. They were not defying Moses. They were simply curious. As members of the priestly tribe of Levites, they wanted to know why God did not speak directly to the people instead of revealing his messages exclusively through Moses and the high priest Aaron—"The Lord told me to tell you this." Korah thought God should want to talk directly to all the people, since they were all his children. Most Protestants today feel that way. Korah said to Moses:

> All the congregation are holy, every one of them, and the Lord is among them. So why then do you exalt yourselves above the assembly of the Lord? (Numbers 16:3)

There is nothing immoral about that question. Nobody was harmed or threatened. This is the same question Martin Luther and John Calvin asked of the pope: "Why do you exalt yourself?" Why do we need intermediaries? In response, God told the other Israelites (through Moses, of course):

> Turn away from the tents of these **wicked** men, and touch nothing of theirs, or you will be swept away for all their sins. (Numbers 16:26)

So in the bible you are "wicked" if you ask your leader to justify his authority. Do modern Christians really think this is a "sin," or that they have "despised the Lord" for questioning their pastor or priest? According to the bible, that's exactly what it is.

> And Moses said . . . "If the Lord creates something new, and the ground opens its mouth and swallows them up, with all that belongs to them, and they go down alive into Sheol, then you shall know that these men have despised the Lord." As soon as he finished speaking all these words, the ground under them was split apart. The earth opened its mouth and

swallowed them up, along with their households—everyone who belonged to Korah and all their goods. So they with all that belonged to them went down alive into Sheol; the earth closed over them, and they perished from the midst of the assembly. (Numbers 16:28–33)

It is from exaggerated tales like these that we get the phrase *of biblical proportions.* The earth-splitting story did not really happen, but it was invented to scare the people into obedience to their religious leaders. Korah's challenge wasn't even disobedience. It was simply questioning the prerogative of those who tell us they are authorized to speak for God. And it got them killed in a fantastic, earth-shaking display of divine anger.

You tell me: where is the evil in that story?

King Saul did something really bad. In *God: The Most Unpleasant Character in All Fiction*, I tell the whole story about what cost him his kingship. What he did was so horrible that God called him "evil" and had him deposed. David then took his place. (If that had not happened, the Jews would have a Star of Saul instead of a Star of David.)

What exactly was Saul's terrible crime? He obeyed orders as he understood them, but not to the complete letter of the law. The genocide God commanded Saul to commit was supposed to be a total annihilation:

Go and attack Amalek, and utterly destroy all that they have;
do not spare them, but kill both man and woman, child and
infant, ox and sheep, camel and donkey. (1 Samuel 15:3)

Saul, a servant of God, eagerly did what he was told. He
obediently massacred an entire people. Or he *thought* that's what
he did.

Saul defeated the Amalekites, from Havilah as far as Shur,
which is east of Egypt. He took King Agag of the Amalekites
alive, but utterly destroyed all the people with the edge of the
sword. (1 Samuel 15:7–8)

This looks like a 100% genocide, and for all practical
purposes, it was. All the men, women, and children were
murdered. But actually, he only committed a 99%+ genocide.
He kept the king alive temporarily, as well as a few animals to
offer as a sacrifice to God.

Saul and the people spared Agag, and the best of the sheep
and of the cattle and of the fatlings, and the lambs, and all
that was valuable, and would not utterly destroy them; all
that was despised and worthless they utterly destroyed. (1
Samuel 15:9)

Notice that Saul, by God's orders, considered innocent
babies and pregnant women to be "despised and utterly
worthless," but a few choice animals were "valuable." The
enraged prophet Samuel asked Saul why he did not kill all of

the animals, as he was expressly ordered.

> Why then did you not obey the voice of the Lord? Why did
> you swoop down on the spoil, and do what was **evil** in the
> sight of the Lord? (1 Samuel 15:19)

Here we see what "evil" really means. Slaughtering families
is good, but *not* following orders to exterminate every single
living being is evil.

"I can explain," Saul protested.

> I have utterly destroyed the Amalekites. But from the spoil the
> people took sheep and cattle, the best of the things devoted
> to destruction, to sacrifice to the Lord your God in Gilgal. (1
> Samuel 15:20–21)

He was going to kill those animals *later*, he said, in a
respectful sacrifice to God. That reasoning wasn't enough to
convince Samuel:

> Has the Lord as great delight in burnt offerings and sacrifices,
> as in obedience to the voice of the Lord? Surely, to obey is
> better than sacrifice . . . Because you have rejected the word
> of the Lord, he has also rejected you from being king. (1
> Samuel 15:22–23)

So, don't worry about morality. Don't concern yourself with
suffering human beings. Kill all the children and their parents
without blinking. Put the master race and the supreme dictator

above everything else. Complete 100% obedience is better than sacrifice. Disobedience is evil, even if you do have (should have) a good reason for it.

The writers of the bible, following orders, were blind to moral principles.

Curses

Preachers often tell us that obeying God leads to blessings, and that is indeed what we find in the opening verses of Deuteronomy 28.

> If you will only obey the Lord your God, by diligently observing all his commandments that I am commanding you today, the Lord your God will set you high above all the nations of the earth; all these blessings shall come upon you and overtake you, if you obey the Lord your God: Blessed shall you be in the city, and blessed shall you be in the field. Blessed shall be the fruit of your womb, the fruit of your ground, and the fruit of your livestock, both the increase of your cattle and the issue of your flock. Blessed shall be your basket and your kneading bowl. Blessed shall you be when you come in, and blessed shall you be when you go out. (Deuteronomy 28:1–6)

That passage continues with eight more verses of blessings (28:7–14), but that's usually where believers end the quote. They like to think of their "loving God" as a provider of goodness.

But notice that it is all conditioned on submission: "If you will only obey." If we keep reading, we see what happens if you *don't* obey. Forsaking God is called "evil."

> But if you will not obey the Lord your God by diligently observing all his commandments and decrees, which I am commanding you today, then all these curses shall come upon you and overtake you: Cursed shall you be in the city, and cursed shall you be in the field. Cursed shall be your basket and your kneading bowl. Cursed shall be the fruit of your womb, the fruit of your ground, the increase of your cattle and the issue of your flock. Cursed shall you be when you come in, and cursed shall you be when you go out. The Lord will send upon you disaster, panic, and frustration in everything you attempt to do, until you are destroyed and perish quickly, on account of the **evil** of your deeds, because you have forsaken me. (Deuteronomy 28:15–20)

How quickly the "loving parent" moves from blessings to curses. Here we see that disobedience is explicitly called "evil." Then there follow not eight, but *forty-eight* verses of additional curses and threats (28:21–68) because of the evil of disobedience. These include pestilence, consumption, fever, inflammation, fiery heat and drought, blight and mildew, military defeat, death ("Your corpses shall be food for every bird of the air and animal of the earth"), boils, ulcers, scurvy, itch ("of which you cannot be healed"), madness, blindness, confusion of mind, abuse, theft of your property, rape of your wife, business failure, abduction of your children, invasion by rapacious foreigners, servitude, humiliation, unproductive crops.

> All these curses shall come upon you, pursuing and overtaking you until you are destroyed, **because you did not obey** the Lord your God, by observing the commandments and the decrees that he commanded you. (Deuteronomy 28:45)

And the threats keep coming: "Because you did not serve the Lord your God joyfully and with gladness of heart," you will suffer additional servitude, hunger, thirst, nakedness, deprivation, and crushing defeat by brutal enemies. As a result of all this punishment for the evil of disobedience, you will be reduced to cannibalism:

> You will eat the fruit of your womb, the flesh of your own sons and daughters whom the Lord your God has given you. Even the most refined and gentle of men among you will begrudge food to his own brother, to the wife whom he embraces, and to the last of his remaining children, giving to none of them any of the flesh of his children whom he is eating, because nothing else remains to him, in the desperate straits to which the enemy siege will reduce you in all your towns. She who is the most refined and gentle among you, so gentle and refined that she does not venture to set the sole of her foot on the ground, will begrudge food to the husband whom she embraces, to her own son, and to her own daughter, begrudging even the afterbirth that comes out from between her thighs, and the children that she bears,

because she is eating them in secret for lack of anything else, in the desperate straits to which the enemy siege will reduce you in your towns. (Deuteronomy 28:53–57)

Imagine reading this passage to Sunday School children. If your family does not obey God, your mother will eat you! And if that is not enough to frighten you into quivering compliance, the chapter continues:

If you do not diligently observe all the words of this law that are written in this book, fearing this glorious and awesome name, the Lord your God, then the Lord will overwhelm both you and your offspring with severe and lasting afflictions and grievous and lasting maladies. (Deuteronomy 28:58–59)

And it gets worse! God broadens the scope of his dominance with an including-but-not-limited-to clause:

Every other malady and affliction, even though not recorded in the book of this law, the Lord will inflict on you until you are destroyed. (Deuteronomy 28:61)

That should do it. If you can imagine it, no matter how horrible, even if not included in this gruesome list, it will happen to you if you don't obey. And this is not just a passive consequence: "the Lord will inflict" his destructive punishment on you, the bible says.

Your life shall hang in doubt before you; night and day you shall be in dread, with no assurance of your life. (Deuteronomy 28:66)

This is not love. This is saying, "I'll be nice to you if you do exactly what I say, otherwise I will destroy you." That's what a kidnapper says to the victim, or what an abusive husband says to his wife.

There are times, of course, when we might choose to obey someone for a good reason. But such obedience needs to be earned, not demanded. If the only way you can gain respect is by frightening your lover with threats and curses, you are not a good lover. You are not moral.

But why should we be surprised? Autocratic government always carries a threat of force. And that force is *itself* evil. Few Christians and Jews realize that their jealous God describes *his own actions* as evil.

God and Evil

We saw in 1 Kings 14:9 that evil is identified with idolatry: "But you have done evil above all those who were before you and have gone and made for yourself other gods . . ."—but if we keep reading we learn that evil is also identified with God himself—". . . therefore, I will bring evil upon the house of Jeroboam" (1 Kings 14:10). It's the same word in the same context in the same passage. According to the bible, God commits evil.

The prophet Isaiah states it most bluntly:

> I am the Lord, and there is none else. I form the light, and create darkness: I make peace, and **create evil**: I the Lord do all these things. (Isaiah 45:7)

Since this verse appears to directly blame God for evil, there have been many attempts to soften its meaning. Besides the King James, at least four other versions (Douay-Rheims, Wycliffe Bible, Jubilee Bible, and Young's Literal Translation) also use "evil" for *ra`ah* in Isaiah 45:7, because that's what it literally means. *Ra`ah* is the same Hebrew word in Genesis 2:9 that refers to the "tree of knowledge of good and evil" in the garden of Eden, and in that case it definitely refers to moral evil—the entire human race is damned because of Eve and Adam's disobedience. But the eighteen other versions I looked up use something different from "evil" in Isaiah 45:7: disaster (5), calamity (4), trouble (3), woe (2), bad (2), doom (1), and sorrow (1). I'm not going to tell translators how to do their jobs. They can certainly invoke poetic license or style preferences, so it's not strictly wrong to have so many different synonyms for *ra`ah*. The direction of the action might make a difference: evil might be one thing when the slave does it, but something else when the slavemaster does it. But it does seem strange to see such a wide variety where the word is so unambiguous in this verse. Why don't any translators call the tree in the Garden of Eden the "tree of knowledge of good and disaster"? In light of the poetic contrasts between the extremes of "light and darkness" in parallel with "peace and evil" in Isaiah 45:7, "evil" does seem to be the right choice. "Evil" is the furthest from "peace" like "darkness" is the furthest from "light." None of the translations have anything other than "darkness" (or "dark") in this verse. They could have substituted "gloom," "dimness," "nighttime," "dusk," "shadow," or "blackness" for *darkness*. But they don't. For *peace*, they could have used "tranquility," "calm," "quiet," "law and order," "harmony," "truce," or "concord." But they don't. They only deviate with the word *evil*.

I think it is obvious why they do this. It's their theology. Most bible translators and most believers think God is good and Satan is evil. The New Testament calls Satan the "evil one." According to Christian theology, God simply cannot be responsible for real evil, metaphysical evil, moral evil, cosmic evil. If we simplistically think of good and evil as cosmic essences, and God and Satan as cosmic opposites, then evil is as far from God as darkness is from light. God's punishments might be described as disaster, calamity, or woe, but God himself cannot be *actually* evil, they are forced to think. The word *evil* in Isaiah 45:7 *has* to refer to something other than what it looks like, according to theology (not linguistics).

But I wonder what difference that makes. Whatever you call it, God openly caused or threatened bad things. Since morality is a question of harm, and the god of the bible is portrayed as causing disaster, calamity, evil, trouble, or woe for no reason other than that his character is offended, then God is immoral. And he seems to admit it. All through scripture, he glories in his power to commit violence.

In *God: The Most Unpleasant Character in All Fiction*, I give more than a thousand examples of the badness of God, a chapter for each of the characteristics in the famous sentence by Richard Dawkins in Chapter 2 of *The God Delusion:*

> The God of the Old Testament is arguably the most unpleasant character in all fiction: jealous and proud of it; a petty, unjust, unforgiving control freak; a vindictive, bloodthirsty ethnic cleanser; a misogynistic, homophobic, racist, infanticidal, genocidal, filicidal, pestilential, megalomaniacal, sadomasochistic, capriciously malevolent bully.

We can't ignore the clear meaning of Isaiah 45:7—God creates evil—but even if we did, there are many other examples of God actually committing evil in scripture. We saw above in Jeremiah 44 how wickedness is equated with idolatry, but notice how God deals with that wickedness. He repays it with evil:

> Thus saith the Lord of hosts, the God of Israel; Ye have seen all the **evil** that I have brought upon Jerusalem . . . Because of their **wickedness** which they have committed to provoke me to anger, in that they went to burn incense, and to serve other gods . . . So that the Lord could no longer bear, because of the **evil** of your doings, and because of the abominations which ye have committed. (Jeremiah 44:2–9,22)

This is tit for tat. Idolatry and disobedience need to be punished. If you do wickedness to me, I will do evil to you.

> Then I contended with the nobles of Judah, and said unto them, What **evil** thing is this that ye do, and profane the sabbath day? Did not your fathers thus, and did not our God bring all this **evil** upon us, and upon this city? yet ye bring more wrath upon Israel by profaning the sabbath. (Nehemiah 13:17–18)

> For the Lord of hosts, that planted thee, hath pronounced **evil** against thee, for the **evil** of the house of Israel and of the house of Judah, which they have done against themselves to provoke me to anger in offering incense unto Baal. (Jeremiah 11:17)

Wherefore hath the Lord pronounced all this **great evil** against us? or what is our iniquity? or what is our sin that we have committed against the Lord our God? . . . Because your fathers have forsaken me, saith the Lord, and have walked after other gods, and have served them, and have worshipped them, and have forsaken me, and have not kept my law. (Jeremiah 16:10–11)

This is like a father telling his child, "If you don't do what I say, I will spank you." Except God's punishment is much worse than a swat on your backside.

And I will lay the dead carcases of the children of Israel before their idols; and I will scatter your bones round about your altars . . . And the slain shall fall in the midst of you, and ye shall know that I am the Lord . . . And they shall know that I am the Lord, and that I have not said in vain that I would do this **evil** unto them. (Ezekiel 6:5–10)

Thus saith the Lord of hosts, the God of Israel; Behold, I will bring **evil** upon this place, the which whosoever heareth, his ears shall tingle . . . And I will cause them to eat the flesh of their sons and the flesh of their daughters, and they shall eat every one the flesh of his friend in the siege. (Jeremiah 19:3–9)

Thus says the Lord, "Behold, I will raise up **evil** against you out of your own house; and I will take your wives before your eyes, and give them to your neighbor, and he shall lie with your wives in the sight of this sun." (2 Samuel 12:11)

So shall it be with all the men that set their faces to go into Egypt to sojourn there; they shall die by the sword, by the famine, and by the pestilence: and none of them shall remain or escape from the **evil** that I will bring upon them. (Jeremiah 42:17)

I the Lord have spoken it. When I shall send upon them the **evil** arrows of famine, which shall be for their destruction, and which I will send to destroy you: and I will increase the famine upon you, and will break your staff of bread: So will I send upon you famine and **evil** beasts, and they shall bereave thee: and pestilence and blood shall pass through thee; and I will bring the sword upon thee. I the Lord have spoken it. (Ezekiel 5:15–17)

For I will cause Elam to be dismayed before their enemies, and before them that seek their life: and I will bring **evil** upon them, even my fierce anger, saith the Lord; and I will send the sword after them, till I have consumed them. (Jeremiah 49:37)

If the child cries as a result of the spanking, that's too bad. God will laugh about it.

Therefore, thus says the Lord, Behold, I am bringing **evil** upon them which they cannot escape; though they cry to me, I will not listen to them. (Jeremiah 11:11)

He [God] destroyeth the perfect and the wicked. If the scourge slay suddenly, he will laugh at the trial of the innocent. The earth is given into the hand of the **wicked**: he covereth the faces of the judges thereof; if not, where, and who is he? (Job 9:22–24)

Although the following words of Job do not use the word *evil*, they do show God himself committing acts of destruction and "iniquity":

How oft is the candle of the wicked put out! and how oft cometh their **destruction** upon them! God distributeth **sorrows** in his anger. They are as stubble before the wind, and as chaff that the storm carrieth away. God layeth up his **iniquity** for his children: he rewardeth him, and he shall know it. His eyes shall see his **destruction**, and he shall drink of the wrath of the Almighty. (Job 21:17–20)

Job, who was being capriciously tortured by God "for no reason" (Job 2:3), openly acknowledged that the terrors he was experiencing were evil acts of God.

Then said his wife unto him, Dost thou still retain thine integrity? curse God, and die. But he said unto her, Thou speakest as one of the foolish women speaketh. What? shall we receive good at the hand of God, and shall we not receive **evil**? In all this did not Job sin with his lips. (Job 2:9–10)

Notice that God brought evil upon Job to tempt him to do wrong, but the temptation was not to cause harm to others. It was to become unfaithful and "sin with his lips." In other words,

Job was being pressured to tell the truth about God's character. The Book of Job is the furthest thing from a moral tale. It has nothing to do with "do unto others." It has to do with bowing to a terrorist.

Job knew he was being tormented by "evil from the Lord," and so did everyone else.

> Then there came to him all his brothers and sisters and all who had known him before, and they ate bread with him in his house; they showed him sympathy and comforted him for all the **evil** that the Lord had brought upon him. (Job 42:11)

Whatever we might think the word *evil* means in any particular verse, the God of the bible seems to wholeheartedly embrace it, and even to brag about it. He uses it as a tool of control.

> For thus says the Lord of hosts: "As I purposed to do **evil** to you, when your fathers provoked me to wrath, and I did not relent, says the Lord of hosts." (Zechariah 8:14)

> Thus saith the Lord, Behold, I will bring **evil** upon this place, and upon the inhabitants thereof, even all the curses that are written in the book which they have read before the king of Judah: Because they have forsaken me, and have burned incense unto other gods. (2 Chronicles 34:24–25)

> And the word of the Lord came to Elijah the Tishbite, saying, Seest thou how Ahab humbleth himself before me? because

he humbleth himself before me, I will not bring the **evil** in his days: but in his son's days will I bring the **evil** upon his house. (1 Kings 21:28–29)

Then my anger will be kindled against them in that day, and I will forsake them and hide my face from them, and they will be devoured; and many **evils** and troubles will come upon them, so that they will say in that day, "Have not these **evils** come upon us because our God is not among us?" (Deuteronomy 31:17)

But God sent an **evil** spirit between Abimelech and the lords of Shechem; and the lords of Shechem dealt treacherously with Abimelech. This happened so that the violence done to the seventy sons of Jerubbaal might be avenged and their blood be laid on their brother Abimelech. (Judges 9:23–24)

Shall a trumpet be blown in the city, and the people not be afraid? Shall there be **evil** in a city, and the Lord hath not done it? (Amos 3:6)

The Lord hath made all things for himself: yea, even the **wicked** for the day of **evil**. (Proverbs 16:4)

Out of the mouth of the most High proceedeth not **evil** and good? (Lamentations 3:38)

Thus says the Lord: Behold, what I have built I am breaking down, and what I have planted I am plucking up—that is, the whole land. And do you seek great things for yourself? Seek them not; for behold, **I am bringing evil upon all flesh**, says the Lord. (Jeremiah, 45:4–5)

It is certainly possible to find verses that say, "God is love." But just quoting those verses out of context, without seeing the broad scope of God's words and actions, tells us little about what that "love" actually entails. There is no question that the god of the bible is wrathful, violent, and evil, controlling his lover with fear and threats. Whenever you hear someone say, "God is love," be sure to point out that that love is conditional, possessive, frightening, hair-trigger angry, and vindictive. I don't know about you, but I would never want to have a relationship with a person who says, "My name is Jealous, and I love you, but if you don't obey me, I will do evil things to you."

Please, love someone else. I want my friends and loved ones to know what morality really means.

Terror

We saw above that Job considered God to be a terrorist. He repeated that accusation more than once:

> For the arrows of the Almighty are in me; my spirit drinks their poison; the **terrors** of God are arrayed against me. (Job 6:4)

> I will teach you by the hand of God: that which is with the Almighty will I not conceal . . . The rich man shall lie down, but he shall not be gathered: he openeth his eyes, and he is not. **Terrors** take hold on him as waters, a tempest stealeth him away in the night. (Job 20:11–20)

> God has made my heart faint; the Almighty has **terrified** me. (Job 23:16)

> **Terrors** are turned upon me: they pursue my soul as the wind. (Job 30:15)

> I was in **terror** of calamity from God. (Job 31:23)

Other biblical writers said the same thing:

A **terror** from God fell upon the cities. (Genesis 35:5)

Enter the caves of the rocks and the holes of the ground, from the **terror** of the Lord, and from the glory of his majesty, when he rises to **terrify** the earth. (Isaiah 2:19)

For thus says the Lord God: Bring up an assembly against them, and make them an object of **terror** and of plunder. The assembly shall stone them and with their swords they shall cut them down; they shall kill their sons and their daughters, and burn up their houses. (Ezekiel 23:46–47)

I will make thee a **terror**, and thou shalt be no more: though thou be sought for, yet shalt thou never be found again, saith the Lord God. (Ezekiel 26:21)

For I have caused my **terror** in the land of the living: and he shall be laid in the midst of the uncircumcised with them that are slain with the sword, even Pharaoh and all his multitude, saith the Lord God. (Ezekiel 32:32)

I will make them an object of **terror** and of plunder. (Psalm 14:5)

Surely thou didst set them in slippery places: thou castedst them down into destruction. How are they brought into desolation, as in a moment! they are utterly consumed with **terrors**. (Psalm 73:18–19)

Lord, why castest thou off my soul? why hidest thou thy face from me? I am afflicted and ready to die from my youth up: while I suffer thy **terrors** I am distracted. Thy fierce wrath goeth over me; thy **terrors** have cut me off. (Psalm 88:14–16)

Knowing therefore the **terror** of the Lord, we persuade men; but we are made manifest unto God; and I trust also are made manifest in your consciences. (Exodus 15:16)

I will send my **terror** in front of you. (Exodus 23:27)

I will bring **terror** on you. (Leviticus 26:16)

Or hath God assayed to go and take him a nation from the midst of another nation, by temptations, by signs, and by wonders, and by war, and by a mighty hand, and by a stretched out arm, and by great **terrors**, according to all that the Lord your God did for you in Egypt before your eyes? (Deuteronomy 4:34)

And when the Lord saw it, he abhorred them . . . And he said, I will hide my face from them . . . I will heap mischiefs upon them . . . The sword without, and **terror** within, shall destroy both the young man and the virgin, the suckling also with the man of gray hairs. (Deuteronomy 32:19–25)

All the great **terror** which Moses shewed in the sight of all Israel. (Deuteronomy 34:12)

And the Lord of hosts shall stir up a scourge for him according to the slaughter of Midian . . . Behold, the Lord, the Lord of hosts, shall lop the bough with **terror**: and the high ones of stature shall be hewn down, and the haughty shall be humbled. (Isaiah 10:26–33)

Hide in the dust from the **terror** of the Lord. (Isaiah 2:10)

Enter the caves of the rocks and the holes of the ground, from the **terror** of the Lord, and from the glory of his majesty, when he rises to terrify the earth. (Isaiah 2:19)

And the land of Judah shall be a **terror** unto Egypt, every one that maketh mention thereof shall be afraid in himself, because of the counsel of the Lord of hosts, which he hath determined against it. (Isaiah 19:17)

Thou hast forsaken me, saith the Lord . . . I will destroy my people since they return not from their ways. Their widows are increased to me above the sand of the seas: I have brought upon them against the mother of the young men a spoiler at noonday: I have caused him to fall upon it suddenly, and **terrors** upon the city. (Jeremiah 15:6–8)

For thus saith the Lord, Behold, I will make thee a **terror** to thyself, and to all thy friends: and they shall fall by the sword of their enemies. (Jeremiah 20:40)

Ah Lord God! behold, thou hast made the heaven and the earth by thy great power and stretched out arm, and there is nothing too hard for thee . . . And hast brought forth thy people Israel out of the land of Egypt with signs, and with wonders, and with a strong hand, and with a stretched out arm, and with great **terror**. (Jeremiah 32:17–20)

Thou hast called as in a solemn day my **terrors** round about, so that in the day of the Lord's anger none escaped nor remained: those that I have swaddled and brought up hath mine enemy consumed. (Lamentations 2:22)

Knowing therefore the **terror** of the Lord, we persuade men; but we are made manifest unto God; and I trust also are made manifest in your consciences. (2 Corinthians 5:11)

There they shall be in great **terror**, in **terror** such as has not been. For God will scatter the bones of the ungodly; they will be put to shame, for God has rejected them. (Psalm 53:5)

They shall be in great **terror**, for God is with the company of the righteous. (Psalms 14:5)

That last verse comes from Psalm 14, which begins by calling atheists fools and ends by calling God a terrorist.

It's not just the bible that displays a morality of violence. The god of the Qu'ran also threatens terror.

Your Lord inspired the angels: "I am with you, so support those who believe. I will cast **terror** into the hearts of those who disbelieve. So strike above the necks, and strike off every fingertip of theirs." (Qu'ran 8:12)

God is your Master, and He is the Best of Helpers. We will throw **terror** into the hearts of those who disbelieve, because they attribute to God partners for which He revealed no sanction. Their lodging is the Fire. Miserable is the lodging of the evildoers. (Qu'ran 3:150–151)

God repelled the disbelievers in their rage; they gained no advantage. God thus spared the believers combat. God is Strong and Mighty. And He brought down from their strongholds those of the People of the Book who backed them, and He threw **terror** into their hearts. Some of them you killed, and others you took captive. (Qu'ran 33:25–26)

Glorifying God is all that exists in the heavens and the earth. He is the Almighty, the Most Wise. It is He who evicted those who disbelieved among the People of the Book from their homes at the first mobilization. You did not think they would leave, and they thought their fortresses would protect them from God. But God came at them from where they never expected, and threw **terror** into their hearts. They wrecked their homes with their own hands, and by the hands of the believers. (Qu'ran 59:1–2)

Lo! Those who chose the calf (for worship), **terror** from their Lord and humiliation will come upon them (Qu'ran 7:152)

The next time you hear about religiously motivated terrorism, remember that its source is to be found in the "morality" of sacred writings.

The New Testament

Thomas Jefferson knew that the bible is a questionable moral guide. In an 1820 letter to William Short, while praising some of the good teachings of Jesus (and denouncing others), he called the laws of Moses "cruel and unjust mummeries" that have no social utility.

> His object was the reformation of some articles in the religion of the Jews, as taught by Moses. That sect had presented for the object of their worship, a being of terrific character, cruel, vindictive, capricious and unjust . . . Moses had bound the Jews to many idle ceremonies, mummeries and observances, of no effect towards producing the social utilities which constitute the essence of virtue . . . the priests of the superstition [were] a blood thirsty race, as cruel and remorseless as the being whom they represented as the family God of Abraham, of Isaac and of Jacob, and the local God of Israel . . . The fumes of the most disordered imaginations were recorded in their religious code, as special communications of the Deity.

The word "terrific" in Jefferson's day meant "terrifying."

The New Testament was a huge missed opportunity. If Jesus had truly been the great moral leader we hear about from the pulpits, he should have taken the opportunity to say, "I apologize for my father. He was a violent sexist jerk." Instead, he said, "The father and I are one" (John 10:30) and "Whoever has seen me has seen the father" (John 14:9). He quoted his jealous father with admiration. Jesus never criticized the bloodthirsty bully of the Hebrew scriptures, never denounced slavery, or punishment with fire. Identifying with his father, Jesus said nonbelievers (those who do not obey his father) would be cast into the fire like branches.

> I am the true vine, and my Father is the vinegrower. He removes every branch in me that bears no fruit . . . Whoever does not abide in me is thrown away like a branch and withers; such branches are gathered, thrown into the fire, and burned. (John 15:1–6)

> Just as the weeds are collected and burned up with fire, so will it be at the end of the age. The Son of Man will send his angels, and they will collect out of his kingdom all causes of sin and all evildoers, and they will throw them into the furnace of fire, where there will be weeping and gnashing of teeth. (Matthew 13:40–42)

> This is the second death, the lake of fire; and anyone whose name was not found written in the book of life was thrown into the lake of fire. (Revelation 20:14–15)

Except for Jesus's fixation on hell, echoing his father's pyromania, and occasional bursts of anger, the New Testament is overall less violent than the Old Testament. The Golden Rule is "new," but it was not new to history because other cultures had expressed it long before. It is new in the sense that there is nothing like a Golden Rule in Old Testament writings, which are concerned only with how the Lord Jealous is treated, not with any true value to human life.

The bible is not the Good Book. It is the God Book.

Responding to the Pharisees, Jesus boiled the Ten Commandments down to Two Commandments,

> "Teacher, which commandment in the law is the greatest?" He said to him, "'You shall love the Lord your God with all your heart, and with all your soul, and with all your mind.' This is the greatest and first commandment. And a second is like it: 'You shall love your neighbor as yourself.' On these two commandments hang all the law and the prophets." (Matthew 22:36–40, repeated in Mark 12:30–31)

Notice that even here—in the kinder, gentler Testament—the love of God comes first, just like it says in the jealous Ten Commandments. Jesus perpetuated the regal attitude that people come second. Looking at the source of the Old Testament verses Jesus was quoting (Deuteronomy 6:4–15 and Leviticus 19:17–18), we see that "love the Lord" was a command to obedience based on fear and threats, and "love your neighbor" meant only "love your Hebrew neighbor."

The New Testament does differ from the Old Testament in some significant ways. The words *evil* and *wicked* are more likely to refer to human-to-human actions in the New Testament, and less likely to refer to God's actions. *Evil* switches from God's actions to the deeds of "the evil one," presumably Satan.

The Greek word most often translated "evil" in the New Testament is *poneros*. Like the Hebrew *ra`ah*, it also has a wide usage, ranging from "annoying" to "ill" to "hurtful" to "bad" to "the Evil One" (as a nominative). It cannot always be understood as metaphysical evil. It sometimes just means "you humans are bad people."

> If you then, who are **evil**, know how to give good gifts to your children, how much more will your Father in heaven give good things to those who ask him! (Matthew 7:11)

Evil is also sometimes connected to bad actions:

> For out of the heart come **evil** intentions, murder, adultery, fornication, theft, false witness, slander. (Matthew 15:19)

The writer of Mark echoes this thought with the Greek word *kakos* (bad) in addition to *poneros*:

> For it is from within, from the human heart, that **evil** intentions come: fornication, theft, murder, adultery, avarice, **wickedness**, deceit, licentiousness, envy, slander, pride, folly. All these **evil** things come from within, and they defile a person. (Mark 7:21–23)

The New Testament sometimes equates "wickedness" with simply being mistaken:

> And when Simon saw that through laying on of the apostles' hands the Holy Ghost was given, he offered them money, Saying, Give me also this power, that on whomsoever I lay hands, he may receive the Holy Ghost. But Peter said unto him, Thy money perish with thee, because thou hast thought that the gift of God may be purchased with money. Thou hast neither part nor lot in this matter: for thy heart is not right in the sight of God. Repent therefore of this thy **wickedness**, and pray God, if perhaps the thought of thine heart may be forgiven thee. (Acts 8:18–22)

> But he answered them, "An **evil** and adulterous generation asks for a sign, but no sign will be given to it except the sign of the prophet Jonah." (Matthew 12:39)

> Then went the Pharisees, and took counsel how they might entangle him in his talk . . . Tell us therefore, What thinkest thou? Is it lawful to give tribute unto Caesar, or not? But Jesus perceived their **wickedness**, and said, Why tempt ye me, ye hypocrites? Show me the tribute money. And they brought unto him a penny. And he saith unto them, Whose is this image and superscription? They say unto him, Caesar's. Then saith he unto them, Render therefore unto Caesar the things which are Caesar's; and unto God the things that are God's. (Matthew 22:15–21)

Evil also refers to simply having "bad thoughts":

But Jesus, perceiving their thoughts, said, "Why do you think **evil** in your hearts?" (Matthew 9:4)

Paul gives us a glimpse of how New Testament writers considered evil:

And since they did not see fit to acknowledge God, God gave them up to a debased mind and to things that should not be done. They were filled with every kind of **wickedness**, **evil**, covetousness, malice. Full of envy, murder, strife, deceit, craftiness, they are gossips, slanderers, God-haters, insolent, haughty, boastful, inventors of **evil**, rebellious toward parents, foolish, faithless, heartless, ruthless. They know God's decree, that those who practice such things deserve to die—yet they not only do them but even applaud others who practice them. (Romans 1:28–32)

In this passage, we do see that *evil* and *wicked*, though dealing mainly with actual human-to-human behavior, are still connected with disobeying God, and are capital crimes deserving of the death penalty. Even if you support capital punishment, I doubt you think boasters and gossipers deserve it.

The bible presents a morality based on threats of punishment, not on minimizing harm. It is not Mere Morality. It is Fear Morality.

Judging God

Bible believers often twist themselves into pretzels to make their "Good Book" look good. They claim that we degenerate humans need absolute morality bestowed upon us from an ethically superior being, but if you actually read the bible you find little to admire about the devious deity depicted in that document.

William Lane Craig is an intelligent and respected Christian debater when it comes to philosophy. His arguments are wrong,[23] but he is not stupid or uninformed. However, when it comes to a discussion of morality, he is truly off the deep end. "In a world without God," Craig writes, "who is to say which values are right and which are wrong? Who is to judge that the values of Adolf Hitler are inferior to those of a saint? The concept of morality loses all meaning in a universe without God . . . For in a universe without God, good and evil do not exist—there is only the bare valueless fact of existence, and there is no one to say you are right and I am wrong."[24] Well, yes there is, Bill. Hitler was wrong because he caused unnecessary harm. And many saints are wrong for the same reason.

During a radio interview replying to my critiques and Sam Harris's denunciations of the genocidal actions of the biblical deity, Craig came to God's defense:

> God is not bound by the same moral duties that we are. Our moral duties are established by God's commandments to us . . . but God himself doesn't issue commands to himself, so he doesn't stand under the same moral duties that we do . . . When God commands the Israelites to exterminate the Canaanite clans, they are acting as God's moral agents under his command. So I think that God had the right to command them to do something which, in the absence of a divine command, would have been wrong, but given a divine command it is not wrong. In fact, it becomes their moral duty.[25]

Genocide is a moral duty? How can Craig know that if it would be wrong to do something "in the absence of a divine command," it is only the divine command that makes it right or wrong? Moral actions, according to Craig, are not determined by real-world consequences: right and wrong come from the decree of the dictator, not from measuring actual harm.

Craig thinks God has a loftier view of what causes harm than we do, so he cannot be judged, but then he goes ahead and judges him:

> Moreover, God had good reason for giving this command. He waited 400 years, while the Israelites were slaves in Egypt, until the Canaanite nation was so wicked, so debauched, that

it was ripe for divine judgment. And so he used the armies of Israel as an instrument of his judgment upon these clans in Canaan, knowing ultimately that their extermination would be better for Israel in the long run—they wouldn't be contaminated by their influences—that these persons were deserving of judgment.

If God can't be judged by human standards, then it shouldn't matter if we think the debauchery of the Canaanites or the genocide of the Israelites is good or evil. If we can't judge God, then it is equally fatuous for us to defend him. It is not up to us to ask for reasons; it is only God who decides. (I'm sure you understand that by talking about "God," I am not agreeing he exists. If I were to say that the Big Bad Wolf is a despicable character, you would know that I am talking about a literary invention, not a real person, who would be bad *if* he existed.) When humans are acting under God's command, according to Craig, then nothing they do can be immoral. If God orders it, the massacre of innocent children is a good and holy act:

I think the hardest thing to understand is how God could command that even the *children* of the Canaanites be slaughtered. But that's why I say God isn't under moral compulsion to prolong anybody's life. If he wants to strike my son or daughter dead, that's his prerogative, and no moral complaint can be raised about that because God isn't under any moral duty to prolong their life, and so he has the right to take the lives of the Canaanite children or to prolong them as he sees fit. And if he uses the Israeli army as his instrument by which he does that, then it seems to me he's perfectly within his rights to do that.

"No moral complaint can be raised" about God? Then why does Craig need to defend his god by claiming that those children were murdered for their own good?

Actually, that's the paradox: the children, by being killed are really, in one sense, better off if we believe children go to heaven, as I do, than they would be, allowing to live on in the circumstances in which they were.

This is despicable. There is no heaven—and Craig certainly does not know if such a place exists—but even if there were, how does it make killing right? (He actually shoots himself in the foot. Craig's reasoning is a good argument for abortion: kill the fetuses now so they can go to heaven without the risk of being raised in a godless family.) This idiocy of theodicy makes a mockery of morality. Under this kind of thinking, *no* action would be wrong. It puts the lie to the Christian claim of moral absolutes. Nothing that humans value dearly, including the lives of our beloved children, would count for squat. No human is capable of acting morally, which turns into a joke the Christian claim that our moral impulses were implanted by God. If you believe that God commanded you to do something that "in the absence of a divine command" would be obviously atrocious, then is such an act actually good? This is moral bankruptcy, but I know exactly where it comes from. It comes from the purpose-driven life whose goal is to bring glory to God. It comes from the toddler morality of pleasing Daddy. The father figure is always right, *must* be always right (he is the father, after all), and to challenge his goodness will hurt his feelings, offend his ego, undermine his authority, and get you in deep trouble. No matter what he does, Daddy is good—God is good, good, good, they have to keep telling themselves.

Those of us who do not saddle ourselves with such perverse purpose—who are no longer toddlers—are free to say to parents and authority figures: "You did wrong." No one can prevent me from exercising my ethical judgment whenever and however I choose. If I think my Dad or the president or the pope screwed up, I will say so. If I think the god character depicted in the bible acted like a monster, I have the freedom and the right to condemn such actions. To do less would be to abdicate moral responsibility.

Blasphemy is a moral impulse.

Blasphemy is insulting or attributing evil intentions to God, which I just did. It is clear why church leaders would invent such a crime. Blasphemy undermines *their* authority. The old joke that "blasphemy is a victimless crime" doesn't go far enough. Blasphemy is no crime at all. It arises from healthy human judgment. When the Church made blasphemy illegal it was actually acknowledging our natural human ethical impulses and rational conclusions. When someone accuses me of blasphemy—and this does happen from time to time—I usually reply: "Wow! Thank you for the compliment!" No authoritarian father can tolerate a bratty child who challenges his commands. Biblical morality says: "Shut up and don't ask questions. God is good, good, good, no matter what you think. God said it, I believe it, and that settles it." No matter what crimes he commands or commits, including gross genocide against human families unknowingly trespassing on his holy property, we are to pretend, against all we consider decent and moral, that "God is love."

So, according to William Lane Craig, if a group of people claims that their god granted them a piece of real estate—a Holy Land—that means they automatically have the moral authority to defend their property by any means against anyone they deem to be "evil." Suppose my brothers and I were to return to our tribe's ancestral land of Manahatta (Manhattan), claiming that our ancient Lenape (Delaware Indian) god had given us that land forever and that the invading Big Apple Tribe of foreign squatters is desecrating our holy sites. The Manetta River was one such site, now completely defiled and paved over, turned into Canal Street. Our ancient trail, which originally followed the high ridge of the island, was broadened into a street of sinfulness. Now marvel in horror at the materialistic debauchery of Broadway! Look at how our sacred holy drumming site has been turned into Washington Square Park, named in honor of an invading warrior, a place where self-destructive drugs are sold and idolatrous music is performed.[26] Gaze at the shocking display of the pagan god Mercury in Rockefeller Center!

As far as I know, my tribe has never hinted at reclaiming our homeland, but imagine if some Delaware Indian warriors were to threaten to set off nuclear devices in the Theater District, claiming that we were sent by our Lenape Lord, "the only true God," to punish the evildoers and cleanse our divinely inherited land of all that is unholy. Would William Lane Craig judge us? On what grounds? If our Lenape Lord told us to reclaim our "holy land," then Craig, by his own logic, would be grossly out of line for criticizing our actions, even if in the absence of a divine command such actions would look reprehensible. If Craig were to object that our genocidal attack would wipe out innocent children, we could simply reply that he, being a fallen non-Lenape human, is incapable of judging our Lenape Lord. It is our solemn duty to follow the orders of the one who issues moral orders. If *you* kill children it is wrong, but if *we* do it under the command of our Supreme American Lawgiver, then it is not only right, it is a sacred honor and a "moral duty." If you object that the holocaust of entire families and neighborhoods is barbaric, I could smugly inform you that you are not in a position to judge the morality because you don't know that those children aren't better off being killed—their souls free to flow eternally down the Manetta River under Canal Street—and spared a much worse fate than if they had to sit through an iniquitous Broadway musical. Our God is good, because he told us he is good. New Yorkers are evil because they are offending his holiness and corrupting our tribe. If you judge our Lenape Lord to be evil, then you are committing blasphemy.

That is all very silly. We are intelligent, caring, rational animals who are capable of assessing harm. Based on his violent genocidal behavior (if he existed), we would have a moral right and a duty to judge Lenape Lord to be a Delaware Demon. For the same reasons, I have a right and a responsibility to judge Yahweh, as described in the bible, to be a moral monster.[27] Of course, the real monsters are those people who commit genocide and violence in the name of their imaginary deities, holding up holiness as a mask for brutality.

In November 2017 I was on national television in Tegucigalpa debating Rev. Carlos Portillo, a former minister of religion in the Honduran government. He told me that since the Honduran people do not trust the government to clean up corruption, and they do trust the clergy, the only practical way to bring morality to the country is through religion. I responded that you can't fix one corruption with another corruption. Religion corrupts moral judgment. When he objected, I pointed to God's ethnic cleansing in the bible, and I asked him, "Is genocide good?" He hesitated for a second, and then on live TV said *"el genocidio es parcialmente bueno"* — genocide is partially good. He could not bring himself to judge God morally. (Nor did he notice that he had just confessed that God is half-bad.) He proved to the world that religion indeed compromises moral judgment.

If we can't judge God to be bad, then neither can we judge him to be good. To worship God is to judge God. If what look like "bad" actions of God might actually be good, then what look like "good" actions of God might actually be bad, and we are helpless to know the difference. When he tells us he is good, he might be lying, and if believers think he is not, they are judging him. If they can judge God, why can't I? They say he is good by his decree. I say he is bad by his actions.

III

Humanistic Morality

Create all the happiness you are able to create; remove all the misery you are able to remove. Every day will allow you—will invite you to add something to the pleasure of others—or to diminish something of their pains.

—Jeremy Bentham, Advise to a young girl
(22 June 1830)

Human Nature

Notice that Christianity has an obverse view of morality: in place of instinct, reason, and an evolving humanistic law, it has original sin, faith, and a divinely revealed absolute law. Many Christians preach a tripartite human nature—body, soul, and spirit—which might map crudely to our three "moral minds." But this framework is doomed to failure since it completely replaces the reason for morality (minimizing harm) with something else, such as following rules or flattering the ego of a dictator whose purpose is to bring glory to himself.

The bible preaches a pessimistic view of human nature. "For all have sinned and come short of the glory of God."[28] There's that intimidating word "glory." Notice that biblical wrongdoing is connected not with real human suffering but with offending the deity. We are all bad: "All have turned away, they have together become worthless; there is no one who does good, not even one."[29] We all deserve to die: "The wages of sin is death."[30] Notice here that death is not viewed as a natural event but as a punishment for the crime of not glorifying the deity. "As in Adam all die, so in Christ shall all be made alive."[31] Without

Jesus, we are all doomed. We are all sinners who deserve eternal torment. We are unable to live a good life on our own because we are corrupted with the original sin transmitted to us through Adam. (I never thought of this when I was a preacher, but if "sin" is inherited, is it genetic?)

A humanistic view of human nature is neither negative nor positive. It is realistic and optimistic. We recognize that we all fall somewhere across a spectrum of characteristics and tendencies that are a mix of violence and empathy. Some will lean more toward "saint" and others toward "sinner," but except for a few people at the far end of the curve who are psychopathic, most of us are neither wholly "bad" nor wholly "good" by nature. We are wholly human. (I put "bad" and "good" in quotes because otherwise they might smack of cosmic judgment, not measurable biological traits.) However, even if we aren't wholly "good" by nature, we have the potential to be wholly moral if we make it a priority to act in ways that minimize harm.

Unlike most believers, most humanists are optimistic about human nature. It's not that we think we are perfect, or even perfectible, but that we can improve. Many individual genetic predispositions cannot be changed, or cannot be changed easily, but this does not mean that an individual cannot control his or her own actions in spite of those tendencies. This is where education, societal expectation, and humanistic law become useful.

Many Christians think humanistic optimism is unwarranted. "Just look at the headlines!" they tell us. "The world is in a mess. We are all sinners. We need a savior." Well, yes, look at the headlines. Those are headlines because they are . . . headlines. Their purpose is to grab attention. They are shocking. They don't reflect normal life. Most of us, fortunately, live our lives outside of the headlines. Think of a horrible story you have read in the newspaper or seen on television. When a mother does something unthinkable to her children or a husband brutalizes his wife, what do you think? When a criminal commits a heinous act, what do you say? If you are like me, you say, "What an inhuman thing to do!" We assume that those violent acts reported in the headlines do *not* reflect basic human nature. We know we are normally kind, empathetic, altruistic, loving, and moral, and *that* is what makes headlines grab our attention. It is good that most people don't make it to those headlines. It is only the extreme deviations from the norm that catch our attention, and they shock us because they are *not* representative of who we really are.

Often we hear sermons announcing that without God we would all be horrible people, stealing, raping, killing, lying. Human nature is hopelessly corrupt. But is it really? If you are a believer, is that how you picture yourself? As you go through the day, are you desperately trying to restrain your malicious impulses? If you could get away with it, would you run around like a maniac, looting, destroying property, sexually assaulting, and causing bodily harm? Don't you simply *know* that such behavior is wrong? Most human beings who want a good life prefer less violence, less harm. Studies show that societies with less religion are better off,[32] so there must be a tendency to a natural goodness that is not in need of divine correction. Since harm is something we biologically want to avoid, most of us are naturally moral. In that sense, I think we can say we are born with "original good," not "original sin."

Sure, you can probably picture yourself acting violently. Each one of us, if pressed hard enough, could be prompted to hurt others. Even the gentlest mother might become a screaming attacker if her children were threatened by a child rapist or murderer. It's not that she desires to cause harm to others but that she might *have* to, to save her children. Self-defense is morally defensible. If your intention is to minimize harm, then you might sometimes have to cause some harm to accomplish that (regrettably or not). I suppose that is part of the equation in the debate to engage in a "just war," if such a concept is meaningful or workable. Even the most ardent pacifists will call the police if there is an intruder in their house, hoping the authorities will arrive with enough show of force to neutralize the threat. Violence is part of the arsenal of survival mechanisms available to us, inherited from our ancestors who managed to escape death long enough to breed and nurture their offspring. But in general, most of us want a life of peace and safety and only view violence as a sometimes unfortunate necessary defensive action, not as a way of life.

Mere Morality is the preference for a world with less harm. Sometimes it is hard to spot the harm in a situation. Is it wrong to cheat on a test? At face value, it would seem that if you can get away with it, cheating on a test hurts no one and gives you a better chance at success in life. But with a little thought the harm becomes clear. If the class is graded on a curve, then by artificially boosting your score you have lowered everyone else's, perhaps dropping another student's grade from one level to another. This difference might be enough to cause that other student to someday lose getting a job when an employer is comparing GPAs on resumes, and that could materially affect their earning potential and their quality of life. On its face, unfairness sometimes doesn't seem to cause much harm, but the consequences in the long run can be significant. If the class is not graded on a curve, there is still the fact that your own GPA becomes inflated, making you appear more qualified to a future employer than you actually are, perhaps causing them to pass by a better candidate for the job. This can affect the profitability of that company, impacting all other employees, harming their lives as a result. If your profession deals with public safety, such as architecture, engineering, or medicine, then the fact that you are overrated can be a real danger to society. If you are the kind of person who cheats on a test, you may also cheat on the job, opening yourself to the possibility of malpractice. (My daughter Sabrina suggested another possible harm from cheating. The professor might alter the test if the curve shifts artificially, causing the next class to find it harder to get a good grade.)

Look for the harm and you will understand morality.

Moral Conflict

Mere Morality cannot determine in advance what is the right behavior in every case. That would turn it into a lifeless formula. We have to figure it out as we go, on our own, depending on the situation. All moral decisions are situational: they need to be evaluated by the context, not by hard-and-fast rules. For example, telling a lie is often harmful, but sometimes it is the right thing to do.

My friend Buzz Kemper, a sound engineer who co-owns Audio for the Arts recording studio and who is the announcer and engineer for Freethought Radio, told me a story about a quick decision he had to make while mountain climbing. Buzz is an experienced climber, having completed ascents as difficult as F5.11 and scaled Devil's Tower numerous times. He was climbing one day with his friend "Bear," who was sometimes a bit skittish and had a tendency to freeze up in fear when things got difficult or dangerous. Buzz was below and Bear was near the top of a moderately difficult ascent when the rope became unsecure and Bear sensed that something might be wrong. "Is everything okay?" he called down. Buzz immediately knew that everything was not okay, that his friend was lacking protection. If Bear slipped, they would both be in serious danger. But Buzz also knew that the remaining short distance to the top was not difficult, so he quickly replied, "Yes, everything is fine. Go ahead." Bear easily scrambled up the rest of the way and waited for Buzz to follow. "It just so happens that I know how his mind works," Buzz said. "While I knew he was more than capable of completing that route if he stayed calm, I also knew that telling him the truth about the situation might have psyched him out, as it would have for me had our positions been reversed." When Buzz got to the top, he told Bear what had happened and admitted that he had lied to him. After a moment's thought, his friend replied, "Thank you. You did the right thing." So far, everyone who has heard this story has agreed with Buzz that telling a lie was the moral thing to do. If he had told the truth, they would have both been at greater risk.

There are no simplistic rules. Life is often messy, and to find the path that is the most moral we usually have to juggle our three moral minds, hoping to arrive at some clarity, or at least a justification for why we think a certain action results in less harm than another. If you recognize that instinct, reason, and humanistic law are useful guides, and then test the results against actual harm, then you are a good person. A good Christian. A good Jew, Hindu, Buddhist, or Muslim. A good atheist. A good human being.

Real ethical dilemmas arise when there is a conflict among our three moral minds. When reason tells you to do something that instinct tells you to avoid, you are at war with yourself. Whatever you do in such a situation is either going to feel bad or appear bad, even if it is the right thing to do. When instinct or reason points you to do something that is against the law, you are at war with society. Sometimes there is no "right" answer. Sometimes we just have to live with who we are and can console ourselves that at least we are doing our best trying to minimize harm.

One of the hypothetical moral dilemmas given in Philosophy 101 classes involves a burning building with children trapped inside. Behind one door are ten screaming kids, and behind the other door is one desperate child. You only have the time or the ability to open one of the doors. Which one do you choose? I think we all agree that reason will direct us to the door with ten children. It would be a horrible choice, knowing that such a decision results in the death of that one child who could have been saved if you had chosen otherwise. But ten is more than one, and based on the principle of minimizing harm, you are justified in rationally directing your action toward the larger group of children, even though you feel a massive reluctance and sorrow at abandoning the one child to its death. No one could fault you for such a decision, and even though you would feel anguished, you should not punish yourself.

Now add one fact to the situation and see if you would act differently. Suppose you realized that the one child was your own son or daughter. All eleven kids are screaming, but your own is calling "Mommy!" or "Daddy!" How would that affect your rational calculations? I am pretty sure you are just like me: you would save your own child first. Rationally it would appear wrong, but instinctively and "morally" it would be right. None of the parents of the other children, though angry and grieving, would fault your decision because they know that they would have done the same thing. Parenting instincts are extremely powerful. Not only are we genetically closer to our children (giving us the evolutionary justification for protecting our own inheritance), but we also know our kids. We love them and they love us. We have spent years with them, singing them lullabies, putting bandages on their scratches, tending to their needs. We know that our own children have come to depend on our personal promise to take care of them. We have looked in their eyes and promised that we will always love and protect them. I challenge you to pretend that you could ignore such a powerful evolutionary tendency to care for your own offspring by mechanically rushing to save the other children first. Parenting is a natural responsibility, after all, that all families recognize and respect.

Even if it were a hundred children, I would still feel the pull of my own child stronger than the others. But I suppose it is possible that if the number were great enough, and if there were enough time to think about it, I would have to consider violating my own instincts and breaking my promise to my own child in order to save the lives of so many others. This would make some evolutionary sense as well, since we all share common genes, and those other children are in my species, and even though I love my own children more, I don't hate any of those other kids. If I were ever forced into making such a decision, I might steel myself and choose the rationally "right" action knowing that it was the instinctively "wrong" action. The right action might require some harm. Under the mental anguish of such a decision, I might then be tempted to end my own life in order to avoid living on with the loss of my own child, hating myself for such a betrayal (and I hope you would try to prevent me from doing that). A parenting instinct is a lens that magnifies the worth of, hence the risk of harm to, our own offspring. Taking everything into account, a moral action is one that intends to minimize harm, sometimes in line with our natural feelings and sometimes in spite of them.

One example of an ethical thought experiment that seems to stump or surprise people is the Trolley Problem.[33] It is indeed an intriguing moral conundrum, but I think the "answer" lies in the fact that reason and instinct are in conflict. I put "answer" in quotes because I don't think there is a correct decision to the dilemma; I think there is a good reason why there is no correct decision.

The basic Trolley Problem goes like this. A runaway trolley is hurtling down the tracks. Ahead, there are five people tied up on the tracks, unable to move out of the way. You are standing by the switch that can divert the train to a different track, but you notice that there is one person tied up on the side track. If you do nothing, five people die. If you move the switch, one person will die. What should you do?

Using reason—the harm principle—most people say they

would move the switch. One person is less than five, and that would be the least amount of overall harm. (Some of those who say they would not move the switch think they can avoid moral responsibility by not getting involved, but I think not acting can be just as much a moral choice as acting.) Using rational calculation alone, moving the switch seems to be the correct answer, the lesser of two evils. I would feel horrible with either decision, but at least I could give a reason for my choice to move the switch.

So far, that is not so difficult. A paradox occurs, however, when the same problem is cast in a slightly different scenario. The same trolley is heading for five people, but this time you are standing on a bridge under which the trolley must pass before hitting the people. An enormously heavy man is standing on the bridge next to you, and you realize that if you push him off, he will stop the trolley and be killed, and you will save the lives of the five people. What do you do?

It seems that using reason—the harm principle—there is no difference between the two scenarios, but most people say they would *not* push the heavy man onto the tracks. Why not? Both scenarios involve taking action to minimize harm. Are the five people less deserving this time? Is the heavy man more deserving than the person tied up on the tracks? Why is one action correct while the equivalent action is incorrect?

I think this is because although the consequences are identical, the actions are not. In the first scenario, although you feel horrible, the one person killed is not so close to you. In the second scenario, you have to physically touch the man and cause his death in a more direct manner. You can't really look away. You are more likely to look in his eyes. He is more likely to communicate fear and disappointment. Your biological instincts toward preserving life are stronger when you are closer to the person. It is more difficult to separate yourself from the harm you are committing (in order to minimize greater harm) when there is nothing separating you from the physical act, such as a mechanical switch. The same kind of instinct that caused me to reach for the falling baby, with no conscious thought, would also cause me to feel revulsion at deliberately causing another human being to fall to his death. The same kind of instinct that causes you to save the life of your own child over the lives of ten children in the burning building would also cause you to feel a kind of moral obligation to the person into whose eyes you are looking.

I'm not saying either decision is ethically correct—to push or not to push—I'm just saying that if you don't push the overweight man onto the tracks, you have a good instinctively moral justification, if not a coldly calculated reason. You probably can't help acting compassionately toward the person in whose eyes you are looking. We wouldn't blame the heavy man himself for not voluntarily jumping, so why should we blame you for not pushing him?

Ethical thought experiments with no clear answer are disturbing, but fortunately, we don't live our lives in such distressing hypothetical emergencies. If we did, we would all have heart attacks from the constant trauma and the species would die out. I think the reason we are uncomfortable with ethical dilemmas is because we think there always *must* be a correct answer. Life doesn't always offer a "correct" answer, and the best we can often do is use the compass of Mere Morality with the intention of heading in the right direction, away from harm, however we perceive it. I think this whole discussion actually underscores the fact that by nature, we are instinctively good animals who are trying our best.

Conclusion

Mere Morality can be summarized like this: using the three moral minds of instinct, law, and reason as guides, try to act with the intention of minimizing harm.

Instinct. When you are confronting a moral decision, first consider how you feel about it. Often, you will simply know what to do, by instinct. I knew I should catch that falling baby even before I knew it. But ancestral impulses can also be wrong in a novel situation, especially in an environment different from the one in which the instinct evolved.

Law. Second, remind yourself what the law says, if anything, about the actions you are contemplating. Many moral dilemmas have nothing to do with the law, but when they do, your society is talking to you. If a law is concerned with minimizing real harm, then it is a good law.

Reason. Third, and most important, use reason to think it through. Reason may override instinct and law that, followed blindly, might cause more harm in a particular situation. Try to be as informed as you can about the results of your actions so that you can weigh the consequences and pick the path that leads to the least amount of overall harm.

And fourth—this is not a moral mind or ethical imperative, but an additional option, a dessert—after having done all of the above, you are welcome to go beyond the minimum of Mere Morality and invest in the lives of others through charity, volunteerism, and compassionate actions. Charity is not an imperative for morality any more than art or music are requirements for society. Acts of kindness that are beyond the moral minimum should be encouraged, but not forced. If you simply avoid causing unnecessary harm, you are passively moral—"merely moral." Charity is a choice, not a duty. If you choose to go further by proactively investing in the well-being of others, you are displaying a character that is truly useful and admirable, and we value you precisely *because* you don't have to do it. If it were expected or demanded, it would not be praiseworthy. It is nice that there are so many individuals— and these include millions of good atheists—who do choose to go beyond Mere Morality to try to make this a world with less violence, more understanding, more beauty, and more happiness.

I smiled when I first heard the question: "If the purpose of life is to make others happy, what is *their* purpose of life?" Helping to make others happy is a good thing, but it is not the purpose of life. Happiness is not something you lack until someone else gives it to you. It's a state of contentment that includes having your basic needs met, sensing you are out of danger, and feeling that you are free to do what you need or want to do. If you can't be happy knowing that others are not, then you are compassionate, and working to lessen the unhappiness of others gives you some purpose in your life. But making others happy is not "the purpose of life." (In *Life Driven Purpose*, I point out that there actually is no purpose *of* life. There is purpose *in* life. As long as there are problems to solve—and there is indeed tragic suffering in the world—there will be purpose in life.) Somewhere, somehow, somebody has to *be* happy, and that is an end in itself. Why shouldn't that somebody be you? And since everybody is a "you," why can't we all strive to be happy and help others to be happy?

My Mom used to say, "If you want to be happy, then be happy." She knew it wasn't that simple, but we understood what she meant. She was almost always singing, humming, smiling, maybe a bit Pollyannaish, but we loved her. She was fun. She knew that we have a lot of control over our decisions, so why not be optimistic? She thought happiness was something we can choose to feel, and maybe that is not true for everybody, but I think we *can* say that about our actions. We can choose to be moral. Instead of making morality a huge mystery, grasping for an "absolute standard" or list of rules or external ethical imperative or purpose-driven motivation or other excuse to treat people nicely, why not simply decide to be reasonable, moral, and kind to others? Paraphrasing my Mom: "If you want to be a good person, then be a good person."

Acknowledgments

I want to thank those who generously gave of their time to read all of parts of the manuscript of this book, or to help me wrestle with concepts during the writing. They include: Philip Appleman, Hector Avalos, Darrell Barker, Geoff Carr, Marie Castle, Rodger Clark, Scott Colson, Jerry Coyne, Richard Dawkins, Jason Eden, Hector A. Garcia, Andrew Gaylor, Annie Laurie Gaylor, Glen (Sabrina) Gaylor, Justin Johnson, Buzz Kemper, David Lambourn, Linda LaScola, Lisa Lee, David Lintner, Lon Ostrander, Gricha Raether, Keith Robertson, Andrew Seidel, Vic Stenger, Phil Stilwell, Gary Thompson, and Larry Thomson. And thank you, Kurt Volkan, for believing in this book.

Notes

1. The name of the cricket in the Disney movie *Pinocchio* was probably picked because "Jiminy Cricket" (mangled from "Jiminy Christmas") was originally a substitute minced oath for "Jesus Christ," the words having the same initials. The Romans used to swear to the god Gemini, and Christians who later wanted to curse but did not want to "take the Lord's name in vain" could say "Gemini Christmas" instead of "Jesus Christ!" ("Jeepers Creepers" is another example.) Further evidence that the Disney writers meant to subtly identify Jiminy Cricket with Christianity are the lyrics paraphrasing Jesus: "Take the straight and narrow path and if you start to slide, give a little whistle."

2. *Mere Christianity*, by C. S. Lewis. In spite of Lewis's valiant attempt to unite Christians, they continue to fight about what should be considered nonessential doctrines, so his argument is moot, persuasive only to a subset of believers. In the chapter "Mere Assertions" in my book *Losing Faith in Faith*, I analyze Lewis's moral argument. In *Godless*, I discuss his famous trilemma—"Jesus was either a lunatic, liar, or Lord"—pointing out that he ignored a fourth option: legend.

3. *Intuition Pumps and Other Tools for Thinking,* by Daniel Dennett.

4. Humanism as a philosophy and way of life is broader than that, but humanistic morality is concerned mainly with harm, as measured against human needs and values. The American Humanist Association has this definition: "Humanism is a progressive philosophy of life that, without theism and other supernatural beliefs, affirms our ability and responsibility to lead ethical lives of personal fulfillment that aspire to the greater good of humanity." The Humanist Manifesto III, talking about "want," "cruelty," "violence," "brutality," and "suffering," contains these words about morality and meaning: "Ethical values are derived from human need and interest as tested by experience. Humanists ground values in human welfare shaped by human circumstances, interests, and concerns and extended to the global ecosystem and beyond. We are committed to treating each person as having inherent worth and dignity, and to making informed choices in a context of freedom consonant with responsibility. Life's fulfillment emerges from individual participation in the service of humane ideals . . . Humanists rely on the rich heritage of human culture and the lifestance of Humanism to provide comfort in times of want and encouragement in times of plenty. Humans are social by nature and find meaning in relationships. Humanists long for and strive toward a world of mutual care and concern, free of cruelty and its consequences, where differences are resolved cooperatively without resorting to violence . . . Working to benefit society maximizes individual happiness. Progressive cultures have worked to free humanity from the brutalities of mere survival and to reduce suffering, improve society, and develop global community. We seek to minimize the inequities of circumstance and ability, and we support a just distribution of nature's resources and the fruits of human effort so that as many as possible can enjoy a good life. Humanists are concerned for the well being of all, are committed to diversity, and respect those of differing yet humane views. We work to uphold the equal enjoyment of human rights and civil liberties in an open, secular society and maintain it is a civic duty to participate in the democratic process and a planetary duty to protect nature's integrity, diversity, and beauty in a secure, sustainable manner."

5. "But he said unto them, All men cannot receive this saying, save they to whom it is given. For there are some eunuchs, which were so born from their mother's womb: and there are some eunuchs, which were made eunuchs of men: and there be eunuchs, which have made themselves eunuchs for the kingdom of heaven's sake. He that is able to receive it, let him receive it." Matthew 19:11–12

6. *On Being Certain: Believing You Are Right Even When You're Not,* by Robert A Burton, M.D.

7. Letter to Thomas Law, June 13, 1814. Notice that Jefferson did not say, "God hath implanted in our breasts a love of others," or "we have been endowed by our Creator with a certain unalienable love for others." Jefferson lived his life as what we might call a "practical atheist," not believing in a personal deity but (as a pre-Darwinian freethinker) assuming there must have been a creative force that started it all, most often equating "God" with "nature."

8. *Descent of Man*, by Charles Darwin, chapter 3.

9. "The Ethical Dog," by Marc Bekoff and Jessica Pierce, *Scientific American Mind*, March/April 2010. The authors discover that canids indeed know how to "play fair," following principles we would call "moral": (1) communicate clearly, (2) mind your manners, (3) admit when you are wrong, (4) be honest. "Violating social norms . . . is not good for perpetuating one's genes," the authors write.

10. Acts of cruelty against other animals are well-known danger signs. Sociopaths, psychopaths, and abusers often escalate from hurting nonhuman animals to hurting human beings. These people are off to the far side of the bell curve. I don't know if this is due mainly to genetics or illness, but I suspect it is a mixture of both.

11. I don't believe in a soul or spirit. The word "soul," as a transcendent entity, has never been defined, so it points to nothing real. If atheists ever use the word, we usually put it in scare quotes and consider it a synonym for something like personality or emotion, which are purely natural.

12. *Why Evolution Is True*, by Jerry Coyne.

13. *The Mind of the Raven*, by Bernd Heinrich.

14. *The Constitutional Code*, by Jeremy Bentham.

15. There is a difference between descriptive laws and prescriptive laws. The laws of nature are descriptive. The laws of society are prescriptive. To say that the laws of society originate in minds is not to say that the laws of nature must also originate in a mind.

16. I actually know something about this. My Dad was an Anaheim police officer for more than twenty years, and while I was in high school I accompanied him to "Skid School" at the station. We studied the coefficients of various road surfaces, related to their type (concrete, asphalt, grass, gravel, dry or wet, etc.), how to estimate the speed of a vehicle at the point when the driver hit the brakes and started skidding across those surfaces (depending on weight and orientation), and how to locate the point of impact from reading skid marks of multiple vehicles before and after impact. The most common thing Dad heard at the scene of an accident was, "I didn't see the other car."

17. I remember hearing Johnny Carson tell a joke on *The Tonight Show* years ago: in California you can rob a bank and shoot the security guards while leaving the building, but when crossing the street be careful not to jaywalk! (Paraphrased from memory).

18. I haven't been able to obtain the recording as of the time of this writing, so I'm paraphrasing from memory.

19. I discuss the inadequacies of the Ten Commandments in depth in *Godless*.

20. Jefferson wrote: "For we know that the common law is that system of law which was introduced by the Saxons on their settlement in England, and altered from time to time by proper legislative authority from that time to the date of Magna Charta, which terminates the period of the common law, or lex non scripta, and commences that of the statute law, or Lex Scripta. This settlement took place about the middle of the fifth century. But Christianity was not introduced till the seventh century; the conversion of the first Christian king of the Heptarchy having taken place about the year 598, and that of the last about 686. Here, then, was a space of two hundred years, during which the common law was in existence, and Christianity no part of it . . . If, therefore, from the settlement of the Saxons to the introduction of Christianity among them, that system of religion could not be a part of the common law, because they were not yet Christians, and if, having their laws from that period to the close of the common law, we are all able to find among them no such act of adoption, we may safely affirm (though contradicted by all the judges and writers on earth) that Christianity neither is, nor ever was a part of the common law." (Thomas Jefferson, "Whether Christianity Is Part of the Common Law?")

21. John F. Kennedy, a Roman Catholic, under accusations that if elected president his allegiance would be more toward Rome than Washington, gave a famous campaign speech to the Greater Houston Ministerial Association in 1960, in which he uttered these famous words: "I believe in an America where the separation of church and state is absolute; where no Catholic prelate would tell the President—should he be Catholic—how to act, and no Protestant minister would tell his parishioners for whom to vote; where no church or church school is granted any public funds or political preference, and where no man is denied public office merely because his religion differs from the President who might appoint him, or the people who might elect him. I believe in an America that is officially neither Catholic, Protestant nor Jewish; where no public official either requests or accept instructions on public policy from the Pope, the National Council of Churches or any other ecclesiastical source; where no religious body seeks to impose its will directly or indirectly upon the general populace or the public acts of its officials, and where religious liberty is so indivisible that an act against one church is treated as an act against all."

22. When Thomas Jefferson was working on the Declaration of Independence, he smudged out a word and replaced it with the word "citizens." It wasn't until recently that scholars were able to use a hyperspectral camera in the Library of Congress to separate out several layers of ink on his draft to read the word underneath. The word he replaced was "subjects." Jefferson had started his draft by copying from the Virginia Constitution (which he had written two months earlier), but then obviously reconsidered what he wanted to say. I think that little smudge was a huge turning point in the history of freedom and democracy, and Jefferson's deliberate rejection of "subject" tells us what was on his mind. We Americans are under no authority but "We, the people." We are not subjects of a king, master, or Lord. See "The World's Memory Keepers," by Steve Marsh, *Delta Sky Magazine*, 2012.

23. I point out the logical flaws, question begging, and equivocations in William Lane Craig's Kalam Argument in my "Cosmological Kalamity" chapter in *Godless*.

24. "The Absurdity of Life Without God," by William Lane Craig, https://www.reasonablefaith.org/.

25. Transcription of "William Lane Craig on Dan Barker and Sam Harris," YouTube, posted by drcraigvideos on August 20, 2009, *youtube.com/watch?v=aQ7C6SVrUjw*.

26. For documentation of the Lenape heritage in Manhattan, see, for example, *Native New Yorkers: The Legacy of the Algonquin People of New York*, by Evan T. Pritchard (Council Oak Books, 2002).

27. The claim that the biblical god is a "moral monster" has been most recently made by Hector Avalos, especially in his chapter "Is Yahweh a Moral Monster?" in *The Christian Delusion: Why Faith Fails* (ed. John W. Loftus), but also in his own book, *Fighting Words: The Origins of Religious Violence*. See also my own book, *GOD: The Most Unpleasant Character in All Fiction*.

28. Romans 3:23. The bible assumes that "sin" is a meaningful wrong, a crime against God. The Greek word for "sin" is *hamartia*, which means "to miss the mark," or to fall short of God's holiness. Since there is no God, it follows that there is no such thing as sin.

29. Romans 3:12

30. Romans 6:23

31. 1 Corinthians 15:22

32. See, for example, *Society Without God*, by Phil Zuckerman.

33. The Trolley Problem was introduced by Philippa Foot in 1967. It was also analyzed by Judith Jarvis Thomson, Peter Unger, and Frances Kamm.

References

Avalos, Hector. *The Bad Jesus: The Ethics of New Testament Ethics.* Sheffield Phoenix Press, 2015.

—————. *Fighting Words: The Origins of Religious Violence.* Prometheus Books, 2005.

Barker, Dan. *Free Will Explained: How Science and Philosophy Converge to Create a Beautiful Illusion.* Sterling Publishing, 2018.

—————. *GOD: The Most Unpleasant Character in All Fiction.* Sterling Publishing, 2016.

—————. *Godless: How an Evangelical Preacher Became One of America's Leading Atheists.* Ulysses Press, 2018.

—————. *Life Driven Purpose: How an Atheist Finds Meaning.* Pitchstone Publishing, 2015.

—————. *Losing Faith in Faith: From Preacher to Atheist.* FFRF, 1992.

—————. *Maybe Right, Maybe Wrong: A Guide for Young Thinkers.* Prometheus Books, 1992.

———. Unpleasant Companion (website), unpleasantgod.ffrf.org.

Bentham, Jeremy. *The Constitutional Code*. 1830.

Bloom, Paul. *Just Babies: The Origins of Good and Evil*. Crown Publishers, 2013.

Burton, Robert A., MD. *On Being Certain: Believing You Are Right Even When You're Not*. St. Martin's Press, 2008.

Coyne, Jeremy. *Why Evolution Is True*. Oxford University Press, 2009.

Darwin, Charles. *Descent of Man*. 1871.

Dawkins, Richard. *The God Delusion*. Houghton Mifflin Harcourt, 2006.

Dennett, Daniel C. *Freedom Evolves*. Viking Adult, 2003.

———. *Intuition Pumps and Other Tools for Thinking*. W. W. Norton & Company, 2013.

Denon, Lester E., ed. *The Bertrand Russell Dictionary of Mind, Matter & Morals*. Citadel Press, 1952. First Carol Publishing, 1993.

De Waal, Frans. *Primates and Philosophers: How Morality Evolved*. Princeton, 2006.

Dugatkin, Lee Alan. *The Altruism Equation: Seven Scientists Search for the Origins of Goodness*. Princeton, 2006.

Ehrman, Bart D. *God's Problem: How the Bible Fails to Answer Our Most Important Question—Why We Suffer*. Harper Collins, 2009.

Epstein, Greg M. *Good Without God: What a Billion Nonreligious People Do Believe*. William Morrow, 2009.

Freud, Sigmund. *The Ego and the Id*. 1923.

Garcia, Hector A. *Alpha God: The Psychology of Religious Violence and Oppression.* Prometheus Books, 2015.

Gazzaniga, Michael S. *The Ethical Brain.* Dana Press, 2005.

Gigerenzer, Gerd. *Gut Feelings: The Intelligence of the Unconscious.* Viking Adult, 2007.

Gladwell, Malcolm. *Blink: The Power of Thinking Without Thinking.* Little, Brown and Company, 2005.

Goldberg, Stuart C. *God on Trial 2000: Indictment of God for Crimes against Job.* PROSCOP, 1999.

Harris, Sam. *The Moral Landscape: How Science Can Determine Human Values.* Free Press, 2010.

Hauser, Marc D. *Moral Minds: The Nature of Right and Wrong.* Harper Perennial, 2006

Heinrich, Bernd. *The Mind of the Raven.* Cliff Street Books, 1999.

Loftus, John W., ed. *The Christian Delusion: Why Faith Fails.* Prometheus Books, 2010.

McGowan, Dale. *Parenting Beyond Belief: On Raising Ethical, Caring Kids Without Religion.* AMACOM, 2011

Nielsen, Kai. *Ethics Without God.* Prometheus Books, 1990.

Packer, Craig. *Into Africa.* University of Chicago Press, 2012.

Pfaff, Donald W. *The Neuroscience of Fair Play: Why We (Usually) Follow the Golden Rule.* Dana Press, 2007.

Ridley, Matt. *The Origins of Virtue: Human Instincts and the Evolution of Cooperation.* Penguin, 1996

Shermer, Michael. *The Moral Arc: How Science Makes Us Better People.* Henry Holt & Company, 2015.

Sinnott-Armstrong, Walter. *Morality: Without God?* Oxford University Press, 2009.

Smith, Tara. *Viable Values: A Study of Life as the Root and Reward of Morality.* Rowan & Littlefield, 2000.

Tremblay, Rodrigue. *The Code for Global Ethics: Ten Humanist Principles.* Prometheus Books, 2010.

Wielenberg, Erik J. *Value and Virtue in a Godless Universe.* Cambridge University Press, 2005.

Wright, Robert. *The Moral Animal: Why We Are the Way We Are: The New Science of Evolutionary Psychology.* Vintage Books, 1994.

Zuckerman, Phil. *Society Without God: What the Least Religious Nations Can Tell Us about Contentment.* NYU Press, 2010.

About the Author

Dan Barker served as an evangelical preacher for nearly 20 years until he decided to leave Christianity. Today he is co-president of the Freedom From Religion Foundation and co-host of Freethought Radio. A widely sought-after lecturer, debater, and performer, he is author of *Godless: How an Evangelical Preacher Became One of America's Leading Atheists*, *Life Driven Purpose: How an Atheist Finds Meaning*, and *GOD: The Most Unpleasant Character in All Fiction*. He lives in Madison, Wisconsin.